THE TRINITY GUIDE
TO ESCHATOLOGY

THE TRINITY GUIDE TO ESCHATOLOGY

William J. La Due

continuum
NEW YORK • LONDON
www.continuumbooks.com

The Continuum International Publishing Group, 15 East 26th Street, New York, NY 10010

The Continuum International Publishing Group Ltd, The Tower Building, 11 York Road, London SE1 7NX

Scripture quotations are taken from the New Revised Standard Version of the Bible, copyright 1989 by the Division of Christian Education of the National Council of the Churches of Christ in the USA. Used by permission.

Cover art: The Resurrection by Sebastiano Ricci © Dulwich Picture Gallery, London by permission of the trustees/SuperStock

Cover design: Corey Kent

Library of Congress Cataloging-in-Publication Data
La Due, William J.
  The Trinity guide to eschatology / William J. La Due.
    p. cm.
  Includes bibliographical references and index.
  ISBN 0-8264-1608-X (pbk.)
  1. Eschatology—History of doctrines. I. Title.
BT819.5.L3 2004
236—dc22
                                                    2003027376

Printed in the United States of America

04 05 06 07 08 09   10 9 8 7 6 5 4 3 2 1

Now hope that is seen is not hope.
For who hopes for what is seen?
But if we hope for what we do not see,
we wait for it with patience.

Romans 8:24–25

CONTENTS

INTRODUCTORY NOTE

It is indeed ironic that our Christian faith provides so little information concerning the life after death. We are asked to believe that the benevolent God will care for us in the future, but the dimensions of that future remain a dark mystery to us. In recent times there has been a marked resurgence of interest in questions relating to eschatology, and this renewed interest has generated a considerable number of studies on the subject. The variety of approaches taken in these works is quite striking and unique when compared with what we find in other theological disciplines in which the boundaries of orthodoxy are more fixed.

After an examination of the biblical and historical data in the realm of Christian eschatology, I have attempted to summarize the thought of twenty-one recent Christian theologians prominent in the field, with a view to making their contributions more accessible to theological students and interested adult readers. I hope that you might take this occasion to clarify and deepen your own faith and hope regarding this crucial subject that must concern us all.

Let me add my sincere thanks to Henry L. Carrigan Jr., my gracious publisher, and to Amy Wagner, the very capable senior managing editor, who have contributed significantly to the realization of this study. Finally, I want to express my profound gratitude to my wife, Margaret, who has been my inspiration and my chief source of encouragement throughout this project.

1

THE BIBLICAL AND HISTORICAL BACKGROUND

The Revelation of the Old Testament

The early history of the Jewish people does not reflect a great deal of faith or confidence in the possibility of life after death. Their concern centered on their unique destiny as a people and their role in the growth of their nation.[1] They did on occasion assert their belief in a kind of thin and shadowy existence beyond death in a place they called Sheol, but this hardly deserved to be considered a fully personal or reflective existence. Their concentration was on the destiny of Israel, although they were always aware that they somehow lived on in their children. Psalm 88 reveals the image of Sheol during the middle years of Jewish history. The occupants of this dark and shadowy place are forsaken—having little hope or recourse. They are remembered no more by the living and are cut off from the Lord's hand as they dwell in the depths of the Pit.[2] After their return from the trauma of the Babylonian exile in the latter half of the sixth century B.C., the Israelites compared their own existence to the shades in Sheol who are depicted as greeting the returnees thus: "You too have become as weak as we! You have become like us!" (Isa 14:10). The sojourn in Babylon allowed the Israelites to be influenced by the teachings of Zoroaster, who lived in Iran in the sixth century B.C. It was he who won over the Persians and the Medes to his faith in the all-powerful god Mazda. The Persians were enamored with spirits or angels who allegedly assisted Mazda in his labors. It was Zoroaster who preached eternal rewards for the good and eternal punishments for the wicked. His theology affected the Israelites and opened them to something more than the lot of Sheol for the dead.[3]

In and after the exile one hears a faint expression of hope for something beyond the confinement of "the Pit." The psalmist ventures some confidence that God will ransom his soul from the power of Sheol (Ps 49:15). However, the author of Ecclesiastes (or Qoheleth),

1

who composed his work circa 300 B.C., holds out no hope whatsoever
for a life beyond death, save for the ghostly lot of those in Sheol who
have "no work or thought or knowledge or wisdom" (Eccles 9:10). He
seems to be a confirmed skeptic who insists that the same fate is allotted both to the good and the evil, the clean and the unclean. The dead
have no reward and "even the memory of them is lost" (Eccles 9:5).
The Wisdom of Solomon, on the other hand, composed probably in
Alexandria in the latter part of the first century B.C., paints a very different picture indeed. God has created humankind for incorruption,
making us in the image of his own eternity (2:23). Whereas the souls
of the virtuous are in the hands of God and no torment will ever touch
them, the wicked and ungodly will be punished. "Their hope is vain,
their labors are unprofitable, and their works are useless" (3:11).

The turning point in Jewish faith regarding afterlife occurred in the
second century B.C. during and after the cruel persecutions of the
Seleucid king, Antiochus IV Epiphanes (175–163 B.C.). It was he who
systematically attempted to rob the Jews of their religion and their culture by forcing upon them Hellenistic images and values. The resistance of the Jews is dutifully recorded in the first and second books of
the Maccabees, which tell the story of Mattathias and his five sons who
heroically organized and pursued the resistance against the Seleucid
attacks. Through the efforts of Judas, Jonathan, and Simon
Maccabeus, the Jews gained their independence, and Simon's son, John
Hyrcanus (135–105) became the first king of the Hasmonian dynasty
that ruled Judea from the period of the Maccabean wars (168–142)
until Pompey occupied the land in 63 B.C.

The prophet Daniel (ca. 160 B.C.) alluded to the possibility of resurrection for those who died fighting the good fight against the
Seleucid persecutors. "Many of those who sleep in the dust of the earth
shall awake, some to everlasting life, and some to shame and everlasting contempt" (Dan 12:2). This represents the first unambiguous reference to resurrection in the Old Testament. Second Maccabees takes
up the theme again, affirming that those brave soldiers who had fallen
in the battles against the Seleucids can be aided by collecting funds and
sending offerings to the temple in Jerusalem so that their sins can be
blotted out.[4] By urging these offerings, Judas Maccabeus "acted very well
and honorably, taking account of the resurrection. For if he were not
expecting that those who had fallen would rise again, it would have
been superfluous and foolish to pray for the dead" (2 Macc 12:43–44).
For the author of 2 Maccabees, the resurrection involves the reunion of
the soul and the body. God's rejuvenated people would then live peacefully

on earth. The resurrection of all the just is apparently assumed. On the other hand, the unjust are to suffer punishment after death, and their bodily resurrection is left in doubt.[5] According to 2 Maccabees, the rewards of the just are seemingly enjoyed shortly after death.

The Revelation of the New Testament

The New Testament evidence regarding the afterlife and the second coming is much more detailed, abundant, and occasionally conflicting. Paul's first letter to the Thessalonians (ca. A.D. 50–51), possibly the earliest of the New Testament writings, contains what some claim to be the clearest statement of the apostle's belief concerning the end time.[6] The risen Christ is depicted as descending from heaven to join the dead who are rising from their resting places to be with the Lord (1 Thess 4:13–18). "Then we who are alive, who are left, will be caught up in the clouds together with them to meet the Lord in the air; and so we will be with the Lord forever" (4:17). As to when this event will occur, Paul declares that the day of the Lord's parousia will come like a thief in the night (5:2). Second Thessalonians, probably written shortly after 1 Thessalonians, teaches that when Jesus returns with his angels, vengeance will be meted out to those who refused to obey the gospel. Their punishment will consist in eternal destruction. In contrast, those who have believed in him will be glorified as his saints (2 Thess 1:7–10).

The next Pauline letter that gives extended attention to the events of the parousia was written several years later (ca. A.D. 54–58). Chapter 15 of 1 Corinthians deals in detail with the post-resurrection appearances of Christ (vv. 3–8) and then stresses the linkage between the resurrection of Jesus and that of believers. Just as all have died in Adam's sin, so all will be made to live again in Christ (v. 22), who will reign until he has defeated all his enemies (v. 25). "When all things are subjected to him, then the Son himself will also be subjected to the one who put all things in subjection under him, so that God may be all in all" (v. 28). When we are raised up, we will possess a spiritual body that replaces our perishable, physical body (v. 44). On the day of the Lord, Paul reminds us that those who have built on the foundation that is Christ will receive an abundant reward. If, however, the labors of some builders are burned up and are of no value, "the builder will suffer loss; the builder will be saved, but only as through fire" (1 Cor 3:15).

In 2 Corinthians, written some months after 1 Corinthians, Paul speaks about being further clothed in the resurrection (5:4). After death there is for him no question of going down to Sheol as a mere ghost without any consciousness or personality.[7] When we die our souls will survive and we will be given a new spiritual body (5:2). Then "all of us must appear before the judgment seat of Christ, so that each may receive recompense for what has been done in the [earthly] body, whether good or evil" (5:10). Paul foresees that he may well die before Christ returns (4:16), but he is confident that even without his earthly body he will be "at home with the Lord" (5:8). In the letter to the Philippians, written circa A.D. 56, Paul speaks of the general resurrection when the Lord "will transform the body of our humiliation that it may be conformed to the body of his glory" (3:21).

Paul touches on the issue of the final outcome of the universe itself in chapter 8 of Romans, written in the winter of A.D. 57–58. The discipline of eschatology not only focuses on the final end of humankind but also deals with the eventual transformation of the world in which we live. Creation itself is longing for its ultimate destiny, eager to be set free "from its bondage to decay" so that it can share one day in "the freedom of the glory of the children of God" (8:21). Paul insists that all of created reality has been "groaning" for liberation and fulfillment, awaiting the day of Christ's return. Incidentally, it is intriguing to note that some Christian scholars over the years, for example, Origen, Gregory of Nyssa, Friedrich Schleiermacher, and Jürgen Moltmann, have found in 1 Corinthians 15:28 the hope—and perhaps even the promise—that ultimately *all* will be subjected to the Son, "so that God may be all in *all*" (emphasis added). This possibility of final universal salvation for every member of the human race seems to represent for some an alternative to the definitive separation of all humankind into the blessed and the damned at the end of time. Some of those who put forward this view as a possibility also point to Romans 5:18: "Just as one man's trespass led to condemnation for *all*, so one man's act of righteousness leads to justification and life for *all*" (emphasis added).

Turning to the Gospels, the good news of Mark leaves us with some confusion regarding the timing of the second coming and the end of days. In one pericope, Jesus announces that some of the disciples will actually be alive when the parousia occurs (9:1), and in another, Christ declares that the gospel must first be announced to all the nations prior to the end of time (13:10) and that only the Father knows when the end time will come (13:32). According to Mark, Jesus warns that it is better to be maimed, losing a hand or an eye, than to be thrown into the unquenchable fire of hell (9:43–48). He promises eternal life to those who follow him and proclaim the good news (10:29–30). To the

Sadducees who tried to trick him with questions regarding the resurrection, Christ replies that the dead will indeed be raised and the good will become like the angels in heaven. The God of the patriarchs is not the God of the dead but of the living (12:18–27).

In Matthew 24, Jesus responds to two questions: (1) the issue of the destruction of the temple and (2) the coming of the parousia. Jesus foretells his return at the end of days (vv. 29–31). He warns of the nearness of the advent of the Son of Man but reminds his disciples that no one really knows the precise day or hour (vv. 36–37). Therefore, they must be vigilant (v. 42).[8] In chapter 25 the evangelist draws a striking portrait of the final judgment (vv. 31–46). When the Son of Man returns at the end of time, all humankind will be gathered before him, with the sheep situated on his right and the goats on his left (vv. 32–33). The sheep will be rewarded with eternal life, while the goats will be sent into eternal punishment. The meaning of "eternal" (aiónios) in this context need not necessarily be interpreted as anything more than a prolonged period of time, although we have customarily defined it as duration without end.[9] The overriding criterion for the separation of the good from the unworthy is the care that we bestow on the poor and the helpless, for as we fail to attend to the needs of the least of our brothers and sisters, we fail to be attentive to Christ.

In the Book of Matthew, Jesus speaks of two paths—one that leads to life and the other to destruction (7:13–14). These alternatives are generally understood as references to the future life. The "kingdom of heaven" and the "outer darkness" are characterized by Jesus as totally divergent destinations for individuals beyond death (8:11–12).[10] He warns us, "Do not fear those who kill the body but cannot kill the soul; rather fear him who can destroy both soul and body in hell" (10:28). Matthew affirms that the future life will involve both the human soul and the body. However, he stresses that while evildoers will experience "weeping and gnashing of teeth" in the furnace of fire, the righteous will "shine like the sun in the kingdom of their Father" (13:42–43). The glorification of the blessed, body and soul, is clearly implied here.

The Gospel of Luke paints several portraits that add new and rich dimensions to Matthew's narrative. The parable of the rich man and Lazarus (16:19–31) reveals the distance between the rich man who died and is tormented in Hades, and poor Lazarus who after death rests in the bosom of Abraham. The divide between them cannot be traversed, even though Lazarus might wish to alleviate the anguish of the once wealthy man with a few refreshing drops of water. Abraham declares, "Between you and us a great chasm has been fixed, so that those who might want to pass from here to you cannot do so, and no one can cross from there to us" (16:26). The implication of the parable is that there seems to be some kind of vague and indirect communication between the souls in Hades and those resting in the bosom of Abraham. The parables of the mustard seed and the yeast (13:18–21) suggest that the coming of the kingdom of God is rather distant because the course of human events must be left to develop slowly over time. Jesus then warns his hearers that those who are saved are relatively few, for the door to the kingdom is narrow and the evildoers will be refused admittance. However, at the same time, he reminds us that men and women "will come from east and west, from north and south, and will eat in the kingdom of God" (13:29). One of the most poignant passages in Luke's Gospel is the story of the good thief who was crucified next to Jesus. "Remember me," he says, "when you come into your kingdom." And Jesus responds, "Today you will be with me in Paradise" (23:42–43).

Unlike the Synoptics, John's Gospel does not contain an apocalyptic portrayal of the end of days. The Lord promises he will go to prepare a place for his disciples, and that he will come again to take them to himself so that they may be with him and remain in his presence (14:3). Jesus does announce that because of him, humankind is divided into those who come into the light and those who refuse to come to him because of their evil deeds (3:18–21). Marie-Emile Boismard emphasizes that for John, those who believe in Jesus will never see death. The soul is indeed immortal, but this immortality, unlike the immortality propounded by Plato, is not a natural quality of the soul but rather a free gift of God.[11] "Everyone who lives and believes in me will never die" (11:26).

The narrative of the resuscitation of Lazarus in John 11 emphasizes the central belief in the resurrection, which is to take place on the last day (v. 24). However, Jesus insists that those who believe in him, even though they die, will still live (v. 25) and in a sense will never die (vv. 25–26). The separation of the soul from the body does not annihilate the individual, for the believer continues to live on. According to Boismard, Jesus seems to sound like Paul because "the realism with which Jesus speaks of our entrance into eternal life leads us to think that for him, the soul does not enter there completely disembodied."[12] In 2 Corinthians 5:1-2 Paul leaves us with the impression that the soul is joined by a heavenly body of some sort as soon as it has left its earthly body behind. "When we have taken it [our earthly body] off, we will not be found naked," but we will be "further clothed" (2 Cor 5:3–4).

This also seems for some, like Boismard, to be the view of Jesus as reflected in the Gospel of John. How this view is reconciled with the general corporeal resurrection on the last day pictured by Matthew remains something of a mystery.

The post-resurrection appearances of Jesus were such that even his disciples did not easily recognize him (Luke 24:16; John 21:12). He appeared as from nowhere and disappeared just as mysteriously. His risen body is glorified, but the nail prints and the wound in his side from the crucifixion are there. What we can deduce from this regarding our own life beyond death remains a dilemma indeed. However, that there will be some sort of continuity between our earthly bodies and our post-resurrection bodies seems to be a given. The picture of bodies being raised from the grave on the last day, which reflects the data in the Synoptics, is somewhat different from the Pauline view in which the soul almost immediately after death receives a new "heavenly dwelling," that is, a new ethereal body.

The destiny of the damned is especially troublesome since they are said to be consigned to Gehenna and its unquenchable fire (Mark 9:43–48). Matthew compares the plight of the evil ones to the weeds of the field after the harvest, when they will be "burned up with fire" at the end of the age (13:40). Whether this means complete destruction or annihilation for the lost souls or endless torture continues to be probed by theologians and biblicists. Edward Schillebeeckx, among others, rejects the notion of eternal suffering for hardened sinners and visualizes their fate as a return to nothingness.[13] After death they would simply cease to exist. This eliminates what Schillebeeckx terms the unimaginable scenario wherein the just enjoy perfect bliss and the unrepentant are tormented with excruciating pain forever. For a good number of thoughtful Christians, this definitive division of the just and the unjust is difficult to imagine, for how can the just be completely happy living with the realization that other members of the human family— also God's children—are hopelessly sentenced to misery without end? For Schillebeeckx and others, considering death as the end of everything for the evil ones is the most acceptable Christian response.[14]

Something must be said about the concluding chapters of the Book of Revelation, which provide us with a symbolic portrait of the final end of the world. The author, whose name is John, in all likelihood composed his work during the final years of the reign of the Roman emperor Domitian (A.D. 81–96), who forced the Christians to worship him as a divinity. Many followers of Christ were martyred, while others, like John, the writer of Revelation, were exiled to deserted places such as the island of Patmos in the Aegean Sea. The purpose of the work, laden with obscure symbolism, was to encourage Christians to keep faith during the time of Domitian's harsh persecution.

In chapter 20 of the Book of Revelation, John sees an angel who lays hold of the dragon (Satan) and throws him into the pit for one thousand years (vv. 2–3). After that period, the devil is to be let out for a time. During those one thousand years, the martyrs of the first century will come to life again to reign with Christ for the millennium (v. 4). The rest of the dead will not return to life until the period of the one thousand years has ended (v. 5). After this millennium, Satan will be released from bondage and will come out to deceive and waylay as many as he can. Fire will then descend from the heavens and consume all the devil's legions, and Satan himself will be thrown into a lake of fire to be tormented forever (vv. 9–10).

At this point God will appear, seated on a great white throne, and before this throne, the dead, great and small, will gather to be judged according to their works (v. 12). All the dead will rise up and be judged according to what they have done (v. 13). Anyone whose name is not found in the Book of Life is dispatched into the lake of fire (v. 15). Then a new heaven and a new earth will appear, and a new Jerusalem will come down from heaven (21:1–2). The home of God will be among mortals. He will be their God and they will be his people (v. 7). This vision of John has been revisited and probed time and time again in subsequent writings, and it constitutes the most significant example of New Testament apocalyptic literature.

Apocalyptic is a rather unique literary genre that usually (but not always) focuses on the events of the end time. The author, who occasionally employs a pseudonym, frequently receives his inspiration in dreams or visions. This type of literature is typically composed in periods of great national or community crisis and is filled with extremely unusual imagery that is difficult to interpret.[15] Some sort of hope is held out for the future after several conflicts and great dangers have passed. The outstanding example of this genre in the Old Testament is the Book of Daniel.

The Historical Development of Eschatology

The Early Fathers and Councils

Eschatology is that area of Christian doctrine concerned with the final destiny of humankind and the world. This discipline focuses on the immortality of the soul, the resurrection of the body, the particular judgment, the second coming of Christ and the new heaven and the new earth, the general judgment at the end of time, purgatory, heaven, and hell.[16] There is both an individual dimension and a cosmic dimension to the study. Over the years, ecclesiastical scholars and church documents have emphasized the individual dimension the most. However, the cosmic dimension, that is, the final outcome of all of created reality, has received considerable attention since the nineteenth century, especially by liberal, political, and liberation theologians.

The subset of cosmic eschatology that has appeared from time to time is the belief called millennialism, which has revealed itself in many guises over the centuries. A somewhat more common version held that shortly before the parousia or second coming of Christ, the world will be afflicted with all sorts of agony, tribulation, and the appearance of the Antichrist. The return of the risen Christ will mark the defeat of the Antichrist. Then the just will be raised from the dead, and a one-thousand-year period of peace and tranquility will occur, during which Christ will reign unchallenged with all the saints. After this Satan and his legions will be released from bondage and the forces of evil will roam the earth for a time. The lost souls will then be raised from their graves and the final judgment will take place. The blessed will be confirmed in grace, while the wicked will be consigned to eternal torment.[17] While the church fathers such as Irenaeus, Justin, Tertullian, and Hippolytus taught several varieties of millennialism, Origen, Jerome, and Augustine refused to give it credence.

A search of the eschatological data from the early Christian tradition leads us initially to the primitive Christian creeds. According to J. N. D. Kelly, one of the first creeds to be formulated and accepted for use by the local bishop was that of the Roman church.[18] Each local community had its own creed that could well be somewhat different in tone from the creeds of nearby churches. This situation persisted up to the Council of Nicaea (325) and even beyond in some locations. The ancient Roman creed preserved by a priest named Tyrannius Rufinus speaks of the risen Christ sitting at the right hand of the Father, from where he will come to judge the living and the dead. Also, the final article of this ancient symbol attests to the resurrection of the flesh.[19] In the primitive initiation rites, those to be baptized were asked to recite portions of the creed in response to a series of questions asked by the baptizing minister. During the ritual, the principal tenets of Christian faith were affirmed by those about to be baptized. According to the historical evidence, the creedal formulas used by the churches in their liturgies remained quite fluid, and the differences from congregation to congregation were often quite apparent.

Among the early church fathers, Justin (d. ca. 165) gives us examples of creeds used in the liturgy that announce the return of Christ to judge all humankind "right back to Adam himself."[20] In the fifth book of his treatise, *Against Heresies,* Irenaeus of Lyons (d. after 200) sets out his millenarian theories in which he describes the resurrection of the just after the destruction of the Antichrist and all his cohorts. Then the just will reign on earth and will receive life with the angels.[21] The new Jerusalem will take shape on earth after it has been revitalized by Christ. Humankind will be renewed so that we can no longer grow old. Those who have lived virtuously will rise first and go to their reward, while those who have traveled down evil ways will experience a resurrection of judgment.

Tertullian (d. after 220) speaks often of a "rule of faith" that has been faithfully handed down by the church, and emphasizes the doctrinal content repeatedly. He speaks about the glorious Lord returning as judge to take the saints into the enjoyment of eternal life while condemning the impious to everlasting fire after all humankind has been raised, body and soul.[22] Origen (d. ca. 254) presents us with a very different view. For him the eventual salvation of all is set out as a hope, although he is not at all sure about the eventual salvation of the devil and his angels.[23] Basing his position largely on 1 Corinthians 15:28, in which God is portrayed as eventually becoming "all in all," Origen argues for the possibility of an ultimate reconciliation of all as the final destiny of the human race.

In the creed adopted by the Council of Nicaea (325) to achieve the greatest possible measure of doctrinal uniformity, little is articulated regarding the last things. Christ is proclaimed as coming again to judge the living and the dead, but no other details are given. The same can be said of the creed of the second ecumenical Council of Constantinople (381) whose symbol bids us to look forward to Christ's return as judge of all, the resurrection of the dead, and the life of the world to come.[24] At Constantinople I, Gregory of Nyssa (d. 395), the younger brother of Basil the Great, was one of the standard bearers of orthodoxy. Although he disagreed with Origen regarding the creation of all human souls before the beginning of time, he did teach that all of humankind will eventually be saved. The just will attain to blessedness soon, whereas the evil ones will have to experience a lengthy purification before entrance into heaven. Catharine Roth summarizes Gregory's position:

So the purificatory suffering must end when this age ends, when all things are restored to their original condition. In fact there is no Hell properly speaking, only a kind of Purgatory. Needless to say, the denial of eternal punishment was one of Gregory's (and Origen's) more controversial ideas.[25]

For Gregory the soul and the body come into being, contrary to Origen's view, at the same time. When one dies the elements of the individual are scattered but the soul remains somehow in connection with them. At the resurrection they will come back together again.[26] The Lord brings about the actual resurrection wherein we experience for the first time the true fullness of our nature. This transformation of our bodily and spiritual nature will occur more quickly for the virtuous and more slowly for the wicked. "The duration of the healing process will undoubtedly be in proportion to the measure of evil which has entered into each person."[27] Our resurrected lives will no longer be governed by our natural properties but will be transformed into a spiritual and unchangeable state. At the conclusion of this age, all of humankind will be restored to God's likeness so that God will be all in all. Before Origen and Gregory of Nyssa, the thesis of universal restoration was also propounded by Clement of Alexandria (d. before 215), one of the first Christian scholars who attempted in his writings to reconcile Christianity and Greek culture. He saw punishment after death as largely medicinal and therefore, not eternal.

Clement can be considered the first Christian exponent of the doctrine of purgatorial suffering; he thus paves the way for centuries of speculation and controversy on the subject of "Purgatory" among Christian theologians. He is also the first Christian writer to suggest, with great caution, the related prospect of universal salvation for all intelligent creatures.[28]

The doctrine of *apokatástasis pantōn* (the final salvation of all) was condemned by canon 9 of the provincial synod of Constantinople in 543. This canon declares that the punishment of the devils and the evil ones is not temporary but everlasting, and those who profess otherwise (i.e., the followers of Origen), are to be considered condemned.[29] Justinian's edict confirming the provincial synod ordered that henceforth no bishop was to be consecrated without his having previously renounced the heresies of Origen and the Origenists.[30] Before the opening of the third ecumenical Council of Constantinople on May 5,

553, the emperor Justinian instructed the bishops who had convened beforehand to deal with the question of the Origenists, which still had not been definitively settled by the provincial synod of 543. The episcopal delegates convoked a special synod and condemned several Origenist positions. The first canon enacted by this special synod reads as follows: "If anyone accepts the mythical preexistence of souls and the monstrous restoration that follows from this *[apokatástasis]*, let him be anathema."[31] This synodal declaration was not considered by the emperor or the bishops as an act of Constantinople II.

Canon 11 of Constantinople II (553) condemned seven heretics along with their writings, and the last of those listed is Origen. The ban covered not only the seven named but also their disciples who propound the same doctrines.[32] The condemnations of 543 and 553 did not in any way diminish the reputation of Gregory of Nyssa in spite of the fact that his view on the eventual salvation of all was quite similar to that of Origen. Some have speculated that it was the pretemporal creation of all human souls and the exaggerations of some of Origen's followers that precipitated the condemnations of Origen. Gregory of Nyssa was consistently honored as a preeminent theologian and saint even during the centuries immediately after his death. Kallistos Ware speculates that if a carefully formulated doctrine of the universal restoration is disassociated from theories about the pretemporal creation of all human souls held by Origen and many of his followers, the theological position holding out the possibility of universal salvation could well be within the range of orthodoxy.[33]

The condemnations of Origen and the Origenists are reflected in the teaching of John of Damascus (d. 749), who brought the patristic age in the East to a close. According to him, after the bodily resurrection the just will share everlasting life with Christ, while the devil, his legions, and the wicked will be dispatched into the eternal fire.[34] Although there is some disagreement regarding the teaching of the eminent seventh-century theologian Maximus the Confessor concerning the matter of universal salvation, the noted patrologist Berthold Altaner has said the following:

> Maximus struggles with the difficult problem of the *apokatás-tasis pantōn* [the salvation of all], and clearly betrays his sympathy with the view that was earlier expounded by Origen and Gregory of Nyssa. Nevertheless he would not have this opinion presented openly and without restraint. Beginners and imperfect Christians should not be led to the abyss of God's

mercy by friendly smiles alone; they must also be guided by fear. . . . This doctrine is reserved for those possessing a profoundly mystical understanding: "We will honor it by silence."[35]

Ambrose (d. 397) the bishop of Milan, was one of the most influential teachers in the Latin church in the fourth century. His views on the nature of punishment beyond death vacillated, however. At times the bishop declares that the tortures of the impious will last forever, and at other times he describes this punishment as entirely medicinal, not unlike the views of Origen and Gregory of Nyssa. Ambrose seems to follow Origen and Gregory also in regard to the theory of universal salvation, which he frequently extends to all humankind. He apparently excludes the devil and his minions from his position concerning the restoration of all and is uncertain whether ordinary souls enter into the joys of heaven immediately after death as do the martyrs and the saints.[36]

Augustine of Hippo (354–430)

Augustine of Hippo has contributed more to the traditional concepts of heaven and hell in the West than any of the other church fathers. He considers the writings of Origen and the Origenists in these matters as little more than a collection of errors and is firm in condemning the thesis of the eventual restoration of all.[37] Immediately after death the impious are dispatched to a region of torment, while the just are delivered to a place of repose and peace. The fallen are subjected to tortures from the time of their death. The just, however, are in a place of rest and enjoy the presence of Christ after they die. The rewards and punishments prior to the final judgment are only a foretaste of what comes thereafter. This increase of happiness or torment is attributed in part to the return of the body after the general resurrection. According to Eugène Portalié, Augustine was the first of the Christian fathers to set out with some precision the teaching concerning purgatorial punishment, and he came close to identifying purgatory as a state of medicinal punishment.[38] The period of purgation after death is deeply affected by the prayers that the living offer for the souls preparing for entrance into eternal happiness. Medicinal punishment was not especially easy for Augustine to comprehend, except that purgatorial punishment is more intense than any of the sufferings experienced on earth. It is allotted to those who die as friends of God but who still must pay for their sinful conduct on earth. After the final judgment all medicinal punishment will have been completed.

Before the final judgment, Augustine teaches that all of humanity will rise, and the same material elements with which one was constituted on earth will somehow come together again. The impious will be made incorruptible so that the fires of hell will not immediately devour them, for otherwise their torment would not be eternal. Augustine emphasizes again and again that the eternity of torment for the damned can in no way be called into question. Although his views on the subject are not entirely clear, the just will not be able to see God before they are rejoined with their risen bodies. He speaks of the just residing in paradise, the bosom of Abraham, or one of the many locations in heaven where they will enjoy the company of Christ and, after the general resurrection, the vision of God.

Augustine lays out his mature vision of the last judgment, heaven, and hell in books 20–22 of his masterpiece *The City of God*, which he composed over a period of some thirteen years and completed about four years before his death.[39] The final judgment, which could take place over several days according to Augustine, will follow upon the resurrection of the dead.[40] The first resurrection is the resurrection out of death, and the second will be realized in the resurrection of the body. The bishop of Hippo refers to damnation as the second death, which follows after the bodily resurrection. The millenarian view, which teaches that there will be a thousand years of peace and tranquillity at the end of world history, is a theory that Augustine admits he once held but later largely abandoned. He does, however, allude to the one-thousand-year reign of Christ along with the just (without their bodies) after six thousand years of human history. The brief return of Satan will occur shortly before the end of time. Then the general resurrection and the last reckoning will follow when Christ will pass judgment on all nations and all people.[41] The bishop of Hippo speaks of the abyss into which "the countless multitude of the wicked are thrust, whose hearts are unfathomably deep in malignity against the church of God."[42] Unfortunately, when the devil returns after the one thousand years of peace, many more will fall away, but the church will finally prevail against him and his minions.

When the day of the corporeal resurrection arrives, the bodies of the wicked will rise up and be condemned to eternal torment. Augustine speaks of the predestination of the just, who with their risen bodies will be taken up into eternal life.[43] After the general judgment, heaven and earth will pass away and a new heaven and a new earth will come into being.[44] Although the saved will know what is transpiring in the regions of the damned, those in hell will not be aware of the boundless happiness of the blessed.[45] The author is confident that great numbers of the Jews who rejected Jesus will in the end return to him.[46]

In book 21 Augustine examines the fate of the damned, and he assures us that the resurrected bodies of the wicked will be so adapted that they can suffer the fiery tortures without ever being consumed.[47] He cites Luke 16:24 in the parable of the rich man and Lazarus to illustrate that hell does indeed involve real fire. After the general judgment, the medicinal or purgatorial sufferings will have ended, but he does allow that the eternal torments will be in some way proportioned to the degree of the sinfulness of the wicked. The bishop of Hippo roundly condemns those like Origen and his followers who speculate that the sufferings of the unjust are only temporary and will some day end so that they too can join the ranks of the saved. He cites Matthew 25:41 and Revelation 20:10 to demonstrate the endlessness of the tortures of hell. For those who have been neither very good nor very evil in their lives, the learned bishop reserves judgment as to their ultimate destiny.[48]

In book 22, the final section of *The City of God,* the Lord is portrayed as bringing together a vast throng of people to fill the void caused by the great multitude of fallen angels who departed with Lucifer. Thus, the heavenly city will still possess its full complement of citizens.[49] Just as Christ rose with the same body he had on earth, so too will all human souls receive back the bodies they possessed during their earthly lives. All will rise in the condition they were in, or would have attained, in their prime. All the blemishes and weaknesses will be gone, and the risen shall be without conflicts or debts of any kind. First John 3:2 promises that the blessed will see God as he is, but whether this means that they will see him with their earthly eyes is not entirely clear.[50] In heaven the body shall move about wherever the spirit wills.[51] Although each will have a share of happiness according to his or her merits, every one of the saved shall possess the gift of contentment to desire no more than he or she possesses. The inhabitants of heaven will be able to recall their earthly lives, their joys and their failings, but will also be able to view the earthly failings and the eternal sufferings of the lost souls who dwell in eternal torment. Augustine's rather cold and fearsome picture of heaven and hell differs markedly from the vision of Gregory of Nyssa and even from that of Ambrose of Milan. For good or ill, however, it was Augustine of Hippo who, more than anyone else, set the tone in the West for the catechesis and preaching regarding the last things.

Another critical source for the development of eschatological thought was the Athanasian Creed. This symbol, which owes more to

Augustine than Athanasius, was probably composed in the fifth or
sixth century by an unknown author in southern Gaul. Gradually this
creed became so influential, especially in the West, that it was almost
placed on a level with the creed of Nicaea and was used frequently in
the liturgy.[52] This rhythmical Latin composition had enormous influence for the rest of the first millennium in the shaping of popular faith
in the West. The creed speaks of the resurrection of all with their bodies
and affirms that all of humankind will be judged on the basis of their
deeds. Although the piece loses much of its lilt in translation, the crisp-
ness and simplicity of the lines make it easy to remember. The concluding passage deals with the final judgment.

> When he [Christ the judge] comes all men will rise with their
> bodies and give account of their deeds, and those who have
> done good will enter into eternal life, while those who have
> done evil into eternal fire. This is the Catholic [Christian] faith.
> And if anyone shall not faithfully and firmly believe it he can-
> not be saved.[53]

The Western Councils to the Reformation

An important creed originating in the West is the profession of faith of
the Fourth Lateran Council in 1215. Its eschatological affirmations are
as follows:

> He [Christ] will come at the end of time to judge the living and
> the dead, to render each according to his works, to the rejected
> as well as the elect; who will also rise with their own bodies
> which they now have so that they may receive according to their
> works, whether they were good or evil, the latter eternal pun-
> ishment with the devil, the former eternal glory with Christ.[54]

A new element enters into the articulation of faith regarding the last
things in a letter written by Pope Innocent IV in 1254 to the bishop of
Tusculum, the papal legate to the Greeks living in southern Italy and
Cyprus. Because these Greeks continued to pray for the dead but were
not prepared to accept any destination between heaven and hell,
Innocent dispatched the following decree:

> And the Greeks are said to believe truly and without doubt
> and to affirm that the souls of those who have undertaken

penance but not completed it, or who die without mortal sin but with venial and minor sins, are cleansed after death and can be helped by the intercession of the Church. Because, however, they [the Greeks] say that the place of purgation has not been shown them with certainty and by name by their teachers, We now wish that that place which according to the tradition and authority of the holy Fathers is called Purgatory should by them also be called by this name. For in that temporary fire, sins not indeed mortal or capital sins not previously remitted by penance, but lesser sins which still weigh upon us although forgiven in this life, are purged. . . . But whoever dies in mortal sin without penance will without any doubt suffer forever in the fires of eternal hell.[55]

This was one of the earliest Christian declarations regarding the existence of a place of medicinal, temporary punishment after death. Innocent IV cites the authority of the church fathers for this declaration. He further affirms that those dying unrepentant in serious sin will be dispatched into the fires of hell.

At the Council of Lyons II (1274), the delegates of the eastern emperor, Michael VIII Paleologus, were asked to commit themselves to the following profession concerning the last things:

And we believe in the true resurrection of this body which we now bear, and in life eternal. . . . But if they [the baptized] die truly repenting in charity before making satisfaction by worthy fruits for what they have done or omitted to do, their souls are purged after death . . . by the punishments of purgation and purification. The intercession of the living faithful is effective in lessening this punishment. . . . But the souls of those who after holy baptism have acquired no stain of sin at all, and those who having incurred the stain of sin are cleansed either while still in the body or after death as described above, are received immediately into heaven. But the souls of those who die in mortal sin or just in original sin go down immediately to hell to be punished, however, by different punishments. . . . [O]n the day of judgment all men will appear before the judgment seat of Christ with their bodies to give an account of their own deeds.[56]

The Greek clergy and faithful, however, were unable to accept these assertions as true statements of their belief. They were considered to be too legalistic and pretentious regarding the state of the departed before the general resurrection. According to John Meyendorff, "The Orthodox Church never entered the road of seeking exact doctrinal statements on the beyond."[57] The decree for the Greeks at the Council of Florence in July 1439 issued the same profession of faith authorized by Lyons II but added that of those in heaven some will see God more perfectly than others depending on their merits. Although this declaration of Lyons II and Florence became a part of the western profession of faith, the Greeks refused to accept it.

In 1336 Pope Benedict XII issued a formal pronouncement concerning the direct vision of God enjoyed by the blessed in heaven. He states that they will see the divine essence face to face and openly as soon as they enter into the kingdom of heaven. They will enjoy this vision until the last judgment and into eternity.[58] The existence of purgatory was confirmed again in 1351 on the occasion of a reunion between Rome and the Armenians. The reality of purgatory was emphasized again as the place where those who die in grace, but who have not yet made complete satisfaction for their sins, reside until their souls are completely cleansed. Then they will be taken into eternal happiness that consists in seeing God face to face.[59] The Tridentine profession of faith issued by Pope Pius IV in 1564 and known as the Tridentine Creed insists once more on the existence of the state of purgatory in which the punishment for past sins is temporary and medicinal.

The Reformers to the Enlightenment

The eschatology of Martin Luther (1483–1546) is absolutely opposed to anything resembling purgatory, but the basic orientation of his thought generally follows the medieval patterns. He describes death as the result of God's anger against humankind.[60] It is seen as the punishment par excellence for human sinfulness. No one views death without agitation and fear. The gospel, however, gives Christians a new approach to death. We are urged to die willingly, and we are able to do so through the power of Christ's death, which transforms death into a kind of "slumber" into which believers move peacefully. The experience of the nonbeliever is quite different, for the terror of such an individual is extreme indeed.

Luther radiates a vigorous conviction that a new life will come forth out of death because of Christ's victory over death. Christ's resurrection is an absolute pledge of the resurrection of all believers. "Everyone who lives and believes in me will never die" (John 11:26). However, Martin

Luther was very critical of all the medieval theorizing concerning the destiny of souls after death, the medicinal punishments, and the offerings to release souls from their torments. His skepticism regarding purgatory and the various degrees of merit to be gained for the suffering souls through good works "arose from the conviction that God would not let himself be pinned down in this way."[61] For him the departed are asleep in the bosom of Christ (or that of Abraham), where they will remain until they are given new bodies when the Lord returns. After death, the souls live on without their bodies in a resting place of some sort, a "halfway house."[62]

At the time of the universal judgment, the souls who have lived in a bodiless state after death will receive their glorified bodies. Luther describes their existence between death and the final judgment as a kind of deep sleep, without consciousness or feeling.[63] For him the intermediate state between death and resurrection is somehow compressed for the individual so that years and years of waiting seem like a matter of hours or minutes. Lutheran theologians in the seventeenth century abandoned his view and returned to the more common medieval tradition, which maintains that after death the disembodied souls enjoy a blissful state with Christ until the final judgment. For them only the body sleeps while the soul remains awake.[64] At the end of time, all the dead, believers and nonbelievers, will rise and appear before the judgment seat of Christ. The evil ones will be dispatched to eternal death and torment, and the believers will enter into eternal life. Luther gives no thought to the eventual redemption of the devil and his legions.

The theology of Martin Luther leaves little room for cosmic eschatology. Although he emphasizes that the end of the world is approaching, eschatological interest in the fate of the cosmos does not occupy much of his attention. However, he does anticipate the eventual restoration of the universe and its completion at the end of time, based on such passages as Romans 8:20ff. He frequently points to the papacy as the embodiment of the Antichrist and to the Catholic Church as the Babylon of the Apocalypse.

> Luther's central presupposition was that history is ultimately the arena in which God and Satan struggle. . . . The severity of Luther's criticism of the pope, as well as his understanding of himself, can be understood only in terms of this view of history. . . . Against this background we can understand what he means when he describes the conflict between the papal

church and the church of the Reformation as the battle between God and Satan.[65]

For him the papacy has set itself above God's Word, "placing the human doctrines of work righteousness in place of the gospel."[66] He consistently refused to draw detailed portraits of the afterlife, for he said, "We know no more about eternal life than children in the womb of their mother know the world they are about to enter."[67]

In book 4 of his frequently edited *Institutes,* John Calvin (1509–64) summarizes his views on the last things.[68] He emphasizes the importance of the bodily resurrection, although it is difficult to believe that bodies long dead will be raised up at the allotted time. The resurrection of Christ and God's omnipotence help us to have faith in our own resurrection. He insists that the happiness of the elect and the punishments of the wicked are eternal. Again and again he warns that it is unwise to be too curious about the soul's intermediate state between death and the final judgment.[69] The just, after their trials and struggles during life, will be taken into "blessed rest," where they will await the promise of glory, but this glory will not be achieved until Christ returns at the end of time.

Then the souls will receive back the original bodies they had during their lives on earth, just as Christ rose with the same body he possessed during his earthly existence. The souls of the wicked after death will be delivered into the torments of hell that they justly deserve, along with their risen bodies. In an instant the dead will be raised up and will be imperishable. We must not trouble ourselves unduly by an immoderate desire to know all the details of our situation after death. "We must be satisfied with the 'mirror' and its 'dimness' until we can see him face to face."[70]

John Calvin was fiercely opposed to the thesis of justification by works, since he saw it as an effort on the part of humans to place obligations on God. He considered this to be the most vicious hypocrisy.

> The most flagrant vehicle of hypocrisy for Calvin was thus justification by works. It included any effort to obligate God, as when "one builds a splendid church, adorns it with rich furnishings, and provides income for saying masses," thinking that thereby "he holds all the keys of the kingdom of heaven so that he can push in even against God's will."[71]

Calvin refers to predestination as God's secret election, which is a mystery he refuses to speculate about.[72] In his judgment, Scripture makes it clear that only a small number out of an incalculable multitude of humankind will win salvation.[73]

> The elect owe to God ceaseless gratitude and full obedience: the reprobate may not question the justice or wisdom of the "dread decree" by which they are left in the state of alienation and damnation. . . . The very discussion of election is a "perilous ocean," and anxiety about it a temptation of Satan.[74]

Although his words engender fear, Calvin was quick to reassure his followers that forgiveness is available to the repentant and that the grace of which they have need will be made available to them.[75]

The seriousness of God's anger against the condemned is made evident again and again. Their torments are described as physical phenomena—unquenchable fire, darkness, and a Gehenna of smoke and confusion. Calvin was convinced that with such images we should be able to picture the lot of the damned. These visions should assist believers who are burdened with the difficulties of life to press forward until Christ is all in all.

In the seventeenth century the general Christian faith understanding regarding the last things remained close to the positions held in western Europe after the Reformation. A small number of saints were thought to achieve heaven, and the wicked—who constituted the majority—were dispatched to hell. The particular judgment immediately after death was clearly affirmed by all, and the universal judgment at the end of time was viewed as necessary because justice must be seen by all to be done.[76] The essence of heaven was thought to be union with God, and in this union all our longings would be satisfied. Preachers and catechists were eloquent in their detailed portrayals of the torments of hell, while there was not so much to recount regarding the joys of heaven. John Milton's *Paradise Regained* was never considered to be as moving and convincing as his *Paradise Lost*. Some even reported that the saints took pleasure in watching the tortures of the wicked in hell.[77] One could estimate that the number of those saved was small because of the worldly and irreligious manner in which great numbers of people lived.

Christian theologians of every persuasion were satisfied that the damnation of nonbelievers was largely the result of their ignorance of the message of Jesus, although some divines did hold out hope for the salvation of virtuous pagans. There were even those who ventured the rather unpopular opinion that the majority of individuals would be saved.

According to historian John McManners, after 1750 or thereabouts attitudes were changing in Europe regarding the tortures of hell, which were beginning to be looked upon as simply incredible.[78] The Calvinists and the Jansenists continued to insist on the stricter line, but more moderate views were becoming rather popular. However, many sincere Christians felt that the maintenance of public morality required a firm hold on the existence of hell.

The Enlightenment to the Nineteenth Century

After the pitched battles over religion in the 1600s, many religious people began to sense that God is too wise and loving to allow humankind to rely on revealed religions, each of which was convinced that the others were false and evil. The harsh wars of religion, with their hatred and carnage, especially in the seventeenth century, paved the way for deism, which became popular in England, France, Germany, and America in the 1700s. Thinkers such as Pierre Bayle (1647–1706), Denis Diderot (1713–84), François Voltaire (1694–1778), and Gotthold Lessing (1729–81) were convinced that the most acceptable approach to Christianity consisted in viewing God as a wise creator who does not intervene at all in the destiny and the affairs of the world. Reason alone is the means whereby God's existence and nature can be discovered through a study of the orderly and consistent operation of the universe.[79] Natural religion fosters no disputes or hatred or wars as do the revealed religions. Furthermore, all the historical religions began at a certain point in time and many die off over the years. On the other hand, natural religion springs from the heart of humankind and is available to all.

Not many Christians in the eighteenth century rejected the possibility of a life beyond death. However, the eternal duration of hell was indeed questioned by a good number. Diderot taught that there was no proportion between eternal punishment and human sin.[80] There was speculation that the souls of the wicked might well be annihilated after death, or that hell might eventually be terminated. An eternal hell came to be viewed by a growing segment of the population in the West as incompatible with the natural goodness of God.[81] Although eighteenth-century theologians and teachers continued to warn believers about the punishments of hell, the threat of an eternity in hell was no longer considered the significant deterrent to immorality that it had been.

Deism came out of England and found a home in France and eventually in Germany. It "begins as a strictly intellectualist system; its aim is to banish mysteries, miracles, and secrets from religion and to expose religion to the light of knowledge [that is, reason]."[82] The leading figures of the Enlightenment were deists in the first half of the eighteenth century, but in the latter half most of them were atheists.[83] It was David Hume (1711–76) who overturned the premises of the natural religion position by demonstrating that the earliest religious experiences among the primitives were polytheistic rather than monotheistic. To assume that human nature is the same everywhere is folly. He considered that human nature is not a treasury of fundamental truths but "a dull confusion of instincts."[84] Hume was convinced that he destroyed the underpinnings of natural religion for all time. Theology gave way to history, law, and natural science as the proper arena of intellectual life.

One very deeply affected by the writings of Hume was Immanuel Kant (1724–1804). It was he who described the Enlightenment as man's leaving his self-caused immaturity. "Have the courage to use your own intelligence!"[85] This directive could be considered a theme of the period. For Kant, pure reason cannot demonstrate the existence of human freedom, the immortality of the human soul, or the existence of God, because these truths transcend the power of reason. However, he readmits them as postulates of practical reason, truths that simply must be assumed so that we can maintain the right order of things. For humans, the pursuit of the perfect good can be realized only through endless progress toward that ideal. This pursuit requires the unending duration of the rational individual moving toward that objective. Thus, the immortality of the human soul is a postulate of the practical reason.[86] Also, the being postulated as the cause of nature must possess intelligence and will and is thus to be conceived as God. It is God who knows our inner life and who is "capable of bringing into existence a world in which happiness is exactly proportioned to virtue."[87] Kant thus reestablished the basis for natural religion by appealing to the postulates of practical reason.

With Jean-Jacques Rousseau (1712–78) we can sense a turn in the thought of the Enlightenment. He not only taught that humankind is good by nature and that death is not the end of human life but also insisted that we are preeminently social beings who must express our feelings to one another. Worship at this time became more animated in many communities. Pietism flourished in Germany among the Moravians, and John Wesley (1703–91) assimilated the Moravian impulses, implanting them in England. Their emphasis was on inward experience and heartfelt common worship. Prayer and song gave vent to human feelings and brought the faithful closer to God.

Friedrich Schleiermacher (1768–1834)

Friedrich Schleiermacher was raised in the spirited Moravian tradition. He was appointed to a professorship at the University of Halle in 1804. In 1807 he moved to Berlin and became minister of Trinity Church, a post he occupied for the remainder of his life. He was appointed to the chair of theology at the University of Berlin and became dean of the faculty in 1810. Four years later Schleiermacher became rector of the university. His masterpiece, *The Christian Faith*, appeared in 1821–22 and was revised by him in 1830. As a compendium of evangelical faith, it is probably the most important summary of Protestant theology produced from the time of the Reformation to the twentieth century. Paragraphs 157–69 deal with the questions relating to eschatology under the rubric of the consummation of the church.[88]

One of Schleiermacher's initial concerns is that God-consciousness exists in all persons, and this consciousness brings with it a belief in personal immortality. However, regarding the nature and dimensions of our personal existence after death, we have no definite knowledge. Schleiermacher advises that the statements on the last things cannot be given the same weight as the doctrines he previously treated. Thus, he calls these observations prophetic doctrines.[89] The first prophetic doctrine deals with the return of Christ who promised that he would once again manifest himself to the world and that this return will occur along with the close of the present state of the universe.[90]

The next observation or doctrine concerns the resurrection of the flesh. Schleiermacher cannot envision human life apart from some bodily component, and he insists that the same personality will be present in persons after the resurrection. This prolongation of the personality of the individual beyond death makes a future life more credible and comprehensible. We are to conceive of the state after death as involving fellowship with Christ, for the thought of a diminished sort of existence does not make sense. The so-called intermediate state between death and the final judgment for the just must therefore be viewed as a state of enhanced perfection.[91]

Schleiermacher holds that the persons in the intermediate state enjoy fellowship with Christ and that they are already in possession of a new body when the soul leaves the old one behind. He has problems, however, in reconciling the notion of the general resurrection with that of the last judgment. It is difficult for him to see how the blessed would not appear after the resurrection in a blessed condition, and if that were the case, what could be the point of the general judgment?[92] These issues, he concludes, must be left in doubt.

The third prophetic observation deals with the final judgment. It is this event that primarily separates the unbelievers from the believers who will enter into a state of total happiness. The complete purification of the souls of the saved, however, will not be achieved at the same time, for the purification of some will take longer than that of others. The blessed will have sympathy for the unbelievers and the rejected, although they will be separated from them. Once the perfecting of the fellowship of the just with Christ has been completed, they will be totally freed from all evil and will enjoy the vision of God and unclouded happiness.[93]

Schleiermacher's fourth prophetic observation deals with what he terms eternal blessedness, which involves the full fellowship of believers with Christ and with each other. For this theologian it seems impossible to envision such a situation without allowing for any inequalities and variations.[94] For him the heavenly vision of God can be described as the complete fullness of a person's God-consciousness. This in no way will do away with our own self-consciousness, and our God-consciousness always remains a mediated reality.[95] Schleiermacher asks whether the blessed experience an unchangeably identical state of happiness or rather an endlessly progressing advance in blessedness. His answer is that we have no response to this question.[96]

Schleiermacher concludes with a brief presentation on the subject of eternal damnation. Can that state be accurately described as one of endless and irremediable misery? He replies that the statements of Christ in the Gospels on this question are not sufficient to support an affirmative response. For him the concept of eternal damnation does not seem to be tenable. He feels that once we posit the existence of eternal bliss for some, eternal damnation for others is inconceivable. Assuming that the blessed would be aware of the torments of the damned after the general judgment, this awareness is bound to tarnish the happiness of the saved. It is possible that the blessed would be acquainted with some of the condemned and thus might conceivably feel some of their guilt.[97]

We should therefore abandon the idea of eternal bliss for some and eternal torment for others, insists Schleiermacher. We do not have irrefutable testimony that this is Christ's design. Such evidence for this position is not at all convincing.

We ought not to retain such an idea without decisive testimony to the fact that it was to this that Christ himself looked forward; and such testimony is wholly lacking. Hence we ought at least to admit the equal rights of the middle view, of which likewise there are traces in the Scriptures [1 Cor 15:26, 55]; the view namely, that through the power of redemption there will one day be a restoration of all souls.[98]

Several years after the death of Schleiermacher, David Friedrich Strauss (1808–74), an assistant lecturer at Tübingen, published his first *Life of Jesus* in 1835. This study made him famous for a brief interval but eventually ruined his prospects for a successful academic career. His work was so shot through with skepticism about the various incidents of Jesus' life that he was removed from his post at Tübingen and was never able to secure a stable university appointment for the remainder of his life. Strauss's findings regarding the history of Jesus as revealed in the Gospels "were so negative that it seemed to many of his readers that he had utterly destroyed the foundations of Christian faith."[99] He reduced much of the historical data to myth, which the early disciples had inserted into the Gospel narratives to enhance Christ's importance in the eyes of believers. For example, Jesus' foreknowledge of some of the events surrounding his passion and death were simply considered by Strauss as details added to the story by his followers who were attempting to improve his image. Because of Strauss's emphasis on a purely critical analysis of incident after incident in the life of Christ, and because of his avoidance of any positive expression of opinion regarding the direction of the narratives, "it is difficult to determine the author's own distinctive conception of the life of Jesus, to discover what he really thinks is moving behind the curtain of myth."[100] Albert Schweitzer was convinced that for Strauss the eschatological passages in the Gospels are the most authentic of all.

If there is anything historic about Jesus, it is his assertion of the claim that in the coming Kingdom He would be manifested as the Son of Man. . . . [I]t is possible that Jesus had a prevision of his death. Perhaps the resolve to die was essential to his Messiahship and he was not forced thereto by circumstances.[101]

The nineteenth century witnessed the publication of an exceptional number of lives of Jesus—mostly by German authors. The majority of these were written from a positivist point of view that avoided the metaphysical questions, for example, the discussion of the relationship between Christ's divinity and his humanity and the nature of his identity with the Father, and focused instead on the events of his life and teachings. There was hope that Jesus could be lifted out of his own time and find his way into the nineteenth century, appearing almost as a contemporary. This according to Schweitzer did not happen. "[He] does not stay; He passes by our time and returns to His own."[102] The theology of the latter nineteenth century, "despite all forced and arbitrary interpretations, could not keep Him in our time, but had to let Him go. He returned to His own time."[103]

An example of this approach is found in the writings of Albrecht Ritschl (1822–89), who taught at the University of Bonn and later at Göttingen. He had little interest in speculative thought, preferring the practical, especially the ethical, dimensions of Christian faith. For him Jesus is divine in the sense that there is "a coincidence of purpose between God and Jesus," giving Jesus a unique relationship to God.[104] The role of Jesus is to establish a worldwide ethical kingdom, which is God's aim as well. For Ritschl the kingdom of God is the final purpose of the world. "The kingdom of God is perfect community with God, and toward this end it energizes an unbroken development of humanity's maturing toward moral perfection."[105] The traditional eschatological issues, the judgment and the final destinies, were not a burning concern for these theologians from Strauss to Ritschl. They concentrated rather on the impact of Christ's teaching and values in this life and on the betterment of the world. Eschatology was a field of endeavor that was relatively unimportant to them.

Albert Schweitzer (1875–1965)

All this changed, however, with Albert Schweitzer, who informed his entire approach to Christian theology with an abiding emphasis on eschatology. In 1901 he published *The Mystery of the Kingdom of God,* which describes in some detail Christ's messianic consciousness and his realization that the coming of the kingdom of God was his special role.[106] After the Twelve returned from their first mission of evangelization, Christ informed them that he would be put to death by the Jews. "Self-humiliation and the meekness of service, such is the new morality of the Kingdom of God which comes into force through Jesus' service unto death."[107] Suffering for Jesus becomes the means of acquiring his messianic authority, and when he formally acknowledges his messianic role before the high priest in Jerusalem, Christ speaks of his return, surrounded by the clouds of heaven (Mark 14:62). "Jesus there-fore sets his death in temporal-causal connection with the eschatologi-cal dawning of the Kingdom."[108]

The ethical demands outlined in the Sermon on the Mount focus on repentance in light of the nearness of the kingdom, and are consid-ered by Schweitzer as an interim ethic making way for the inbreak of the kingdom. It is a set of moral demands "oriented entirely by the expected supernatural consummation."[109] According to Schweitzer, it was at his baptism that Christ became conscious of his messianic iden-tity. This secret he shared with his disciples on the occasion of their visit to Caesarea Philippi (Mark 8:27–30), although he insisted that they reveal this fact to no one. It was not until his formal encounter with the high priest in Jerusalem that he publicly acknowledged that he was the Messiah (Mark 14:60–62). Even during Jesus' final entrance into Jerusalem, he was acclaimed not as the Messiah but as the forerunner who was to precede the Messiah. Jesus had always preferred the title "Son of Man" because it "refers to the moment in which the Messiah shall come upon the clouds of heaven for judgment."[110] Only on that messianic day would Jesus appear as the Son of Man.

In Schweitzer's view the resurrection of the dead is to precede the establishment of the kingdom. All those who have died will gather before the judgment seat, while those who are alive at that moment will be transformed and will stand with those who have been raised from the dead. Jesus will then come upon the clouds to usher in the mes-sianic epoch.[111] And it is after the general judgment that the kingdom will dawn. Jesus came to see himself as the Suffering Servant of 2 Isaiah who was to atone for the sins of others. "His appearing and his procla-mation have to do only with the near approach of the Kingdom."[112] The sending out of the Twelve was, according to Schweitzer, the final effort to bring about the coming of the kingdom (Mark 6:7–13). When they returned with the stories of their missionary successes, Jesus was convinced that the kingdom was near at hand. However, the king-dom failed to appear. It became clear to him that he must go to Jerusalem to confront his enemies and there be put to death in order that the kingdom and the messianic age might break through.

Schweitzer, in his second and more celebrated volume, *The Quest of the Historical Jesus* (1906), reiterates his message of consistent eschatol-ogy, insisting that Jesus' life and activity are based exclusively on the imminent expectation of the kingdom of God.[113] According to Schweitzer, the roughly seventy nineteenth-century lives of Jesus he analyzes in this study made Jesus "too small" and adapted him to our human standards and psychology. He became "a figure designed by rationalism, endowed with life by liberalism, and clothed by modern [nineteenth-century] theology in a historical garb."[114] To Schweitzer Jesus was infinitely more than this. At the core of Christ's message was his constant preaching concerning the eschatological kingdom that he thought would be ushered in through his person and death.

Observations

The Jewish notions concerning the afterlife seem to clarify and become more explicit in the second century B.C. The Books of Daniel and the Maccabees refer to the blessed resurrection of the just, while the unjust are to suffer punishment after death. In the New Testament we encounter abundant evidence regarding the afterlife. Paul's letters give us a good deal of information concerning Christ's resurrection as a pledge of our own resurrection, and the spiritual bodies that we will receive. The final judgment will allot to us the recompense that our lives have deserved, whether good or evil. The Gospels also speak of the two paths—one that leads to life and the other to destruction. Whether the term *aiónios* (eternal) means endless banishment or only a long period of time is not clear in the Scriptures.

The Fathers of the early church wrestled with such issues as the duration of medicinal penalties, and even the possibility of the eventual salvation of all. It was Augustine (354–430), however, who gave expression to the rigid concepts of heaven, purgation, and hell that have survived as the common teaching in the West. In the mid-eighteenth century the culture of the Enlightenment began to move away somewhat from the notion of an eternal hell for the unjust, and lifted up a hope that somehow all would be saved eventually. But in spite of this, the traditional tenets of salvation for some and damnation for others have remained the prevailing popular teaching.

NOTES

1. "The Old Testament is then seen as the key source for the explanation of the life and death of a people, just as the New Testament became the literary key source for the explanation of Jesus' life and death." Edward Schillebeeckx, "The Interpretation of Eschatology," *Concilium* 41 (1969): 43.

2. Ps 88:4–6. All biblical citations and quotations are taken from *The New Oxford Annotated Bible with the Apocrypha: New Revised*

Standard Version (ed. Bruce M. Metzger and Roland E. Murphy; New York: Oxford University Press, 1991).

3. Lawrence Boadt, *Reading the Old Testament* (New York: Paulist Press, 1984), 433.

4. Second Maccabees was written in Greek between 104 and 63 B.C.

5. André-Marie Dubarle, "Belief in Immortality in the Old Testament and Judaism," *Concilium* 66 (1970): 44.

6. See James D. G. Dunn, *The Theology of Paul the Apostle* (Grand Rapids: Eerdmans, 1998), 299.

7. Marie-Emile Boismard, *Our Victory over Death: Resurrection?* (trans. Madeleine Beaumont; Collegeville, Minn.: Liturgical Press, 1999), 89.

8. Ulrich Luz, *The Theology of the Gospel of Matthew* (trans. J. Bradford Robinson; Cambridge: Cambridge University Press, 1996), 125–32.

9. *Theological Dictionary of the New Testament* (ed. Gerhard Kittel and Gerhard Friedrich; abridged in one vol. by Geoffrey W. Bromiley; Grand Rapids: Eerdmans, 1985; repr. 1990), 31–32.

10. Franz Mussner, "The Synoptic Account of Jesus' Teaching on the Future Life," *Concilium* 66 (1970): 46.

11. Boismard, *Our Victory over Death*, 120.

12. Ibid.

13. Edward Schillebeeckx, *Church: The Human Story of God* (trans. John Bowden; New York: Crossroad, 1990), 137.

14. Ibid., 138.

15. James D. G. Dunn, *Unity and Diversity in the New Testament* (2d ed.; London: SCM Press, 1990), 310–15.

16. Van A. Harvey, *A Handbook of Theological Terms* (New York: Macmillan, 1964), 80.

17. Ibid., 80–81.

18. J. N. D. Kelly, *Early Christian Creeds* (3d ed.; New York: Longman, 1972), 101.

19. Ibid., 102.

20. Ibid., 75.

21. Robert M. Grant, *Irenaeus of Lyons* (New York: Routledge, 1997), 182.

22. Kelly, *Early Christian Creeds*, 85.

23. Kallistos Ware, *The Inner Kingdom*, vol. 1 of *The Collected Works* (Crestwood, N.Y.: St. Vladimir's Seminary Press, 2000), 200–202.

24. Kelly, *Early Christian Creeds*, 297–98.

25. Gregory of Nyssa, *On the Soul and the Resurrection* (trans. Catharine P. Roth; Crestwood, N.Y.: St. Vladimir's Seminary Press, 1993), 19.

26. Ibid., 103.

27. Ibid., 116.

28. Brian E. Daley, *The Hope of the Early Church: A Handbook of Patristic Eschatology* (Cambridge: Cambridge University Press, 1991), 44ff.

29. Josef Neuner and Heinrich Roos, *The Teaching of the Catholic Church* (ed. Karl Rahner, trans. Geoffrey Stevens; New York: Alba House, 1967), 415.

30. Aloys Grillmeier and Theresia Hainthaler, *Christ in Christian Tradition* (vol. 2, pt. 2; trans. Pauline Allen and John Cawte; Louisville, Ky.: Westminster John Knox, 1995), 392.

31. Ibid., 404.

32. Giuseppe Alberigo et al. *Decrees of the Ecumenical Councils* (vol. 1; ed. N. Tanner; Washington, D.C.: Georgetown University Press, 1990), *119.

33. Ware, *The Inner Kingdom*, 206.

34. Daley, *Hope of the Early Church*, 203.

35. Berthold Altaner, *Patrology* (trans. Hilda C. Graef; New York: Herder & Herder, 1960), 632. Brian Daley disagrees with Altaner's reading of Maximus in this regard. Cf. Daley, *Hope of the Early Church*, 202.

36. Daley, 97–101.

37. For a valuable summary of Augustine's eschatology, see Eugène Portalié, *A Guide to the Thought of Saint Augustine* (trans. Ralph J. Bastian; Westport, Conn.: Greenwood Press, 1960), 289–304. This study is a translation of Portalié's article on Augustine in the *Dictionnaire de théologie catholique*.

38. Ibid., 295.

39. Augustine, *The City of God* (trans. Marcus Dods; New York: Random House, 1950).

40. Ibid., 715.

41. Ibid.

42. Ibid., 720.

43. Ibid., 735.

44. Ibid., 732.

45. Ibid., 747.

46. Ibid., 758.

47. Ibid., 776.

48. Ibid., 809.

49. Ibid., 811.

50. Ibid., 861.

51. Ibid., 864.

52. H. Denzinger and A. Schönmetzer, *Enchiridion Symbolorum* (32d ed.; Freiburg: Herder, 1963), nos. 75–76.

53. Neuner and Roos, *Teaching of the Catholic Church,* 429.

54. Ibid., 431.

55. Ibid., 417–18.

56. Ibid., 433–34.

57. John Meyendorff, *Byzantine Theology* (2d ed.; New York: Fordham University Press, 1987), 221.

58. Neuner and Roos, *Teaching of the Catholic Church,* 419–20.

59. Ibid., 421.

60. Luther's thought as summarized here is to be found in Paul Althaus, *The Theology of Martin Luther* (Philadelphia: Fortress, 1966), 404–25.

61. Heiko A. Oberman, *Luther: Man between God and the Devil* (trans. Eileen Walliser-Schwarzbart; New Haven, Conn.: Yale University Press, 1989), 147.

62. Althaus, *Theology of Martin Luther,* 413.

63. Ibid., 415.

64. Ibid., 417.

65. Bernhard Lohse, *Martin Luther: An Introduction to His Life and Work* (trans. Robert C. Schultz; Philadelphia: Fortress, 1986), 195.

66. Althaus, *Theology of Martin Luther,* 420.

67. Ibid., 425.

68. *Calvin's Institutes: A New Compend* (ed. Hugh T. Kerr; Louisville, Ky.: Westminster John Knox, 1989), 120–26.

69. Ibid., 124.

70. Ibid., 125.

71. William Bouwsma, *John Calvin: A Sixteenth-Century Portrait* (New York: Oxford University Press, 1988), 62.

72. Ibid., 173.

73. Ibid.

74. John T. McNeill, *The History and Character of Calvinism* (Oxford: Oxford University Press, 1967), 211.

75. Ibid., 212.

76. John McManners, *Death and Enlightenment* (New York: Oxford University Press, 1981), 129.

77. Ibid., 136.

78. Ibid., 143.

79. Harvey, *Handbook of Theological Terms,* 66.

80. McManners, *Death and Enlightenment,* 184.

81. Ibid., 177.

82. Ernst Cassirer, *The Philosophy of the Enlightenment* (trans. Fritz C. A. Koelln and James P. Pettegrove; Princeton, N.J.: Princeton University Press, 1979), 171.

83. Peter Gay, *The Enlightenment: The Rise of Modern Paganism* (New York: W. W. Norton, 1966), 18.

84. Cassirer, *Philosophy of the Enlightenment*, 178.

85. Immanuel Kant, "What Is the Enlightenment?" *The Philosophy of Kant: Immanuel Kant's Moral and Political Writings* (ed. Carl J. Friedrich; New York: Random House, 1949; repr. 1977), 132–33.

86. Frederick Copleston, *A History of Philosophy* (bk. 2, vols. 4–6; 1st ed. 1963–64; repr., Garden City, N.Y.: Image Books, 1985), 338.

87. Ibid., 340.

88. Friedrich Schleiermacher, *The Christian Faith* (trans. from the 2d German ed. by H. R. MacKintosh and J. S. Stewart; Edinburgh: T&T Clark, 1986), 696–737.

89. Ibid., 705

90. Ibid., 708.

91. Ibid., 712.

92. Ibid., 713.

93. Ibid., 716–17.

94. Ibid., 718.

95. Ibid., 719.

96. Ibid., 720.

97. Ibid., 721.

98. Ibid., 722.

99. John Macquarrie, *Jesus Christ in Modern Thought* (Philadelphia: Trinity Press International, 1990), 225.

100. Albert Schweitzer, *The Quest of the Historical Jesus* (trans. W. Montgomery; New York: Macmillan, 1968), 90.

101. Ibid., 94–95.

102. Ibid., 399.

103. Ibid.

104. Macquarrie, *Jesus Christ in Modern Thought*, 256.

105. Gerhard Sauter, *What Dare We Hope?* (Harrisburg, Pa.: Trinity Press International, 1999), 27.

106. Albert Schweitzer, *The Mystery of the Kingdom of God* (trans. Walter Lowrie; London: Adam & Charles Black, 1956).

107. Ibid., 73–74.

108. Ibid., 80.

109. Ibid., 100.
110. Ibid., 191.
111. Ibid., 208.
112. Ibid., 254.
113. Sauter, *What Dare We Hope?*, 32.
114. Schweitzer, *Quest of the Historical Jesus*, 398.

2

BULTMANN, CULLMANN, AND TILLICH: CLASSIC PROTESTANT APPROACHES TO ESCHATOLOGY IN THE TWENTIETH CENTURY

Rudolf Bultmann (1884–1976)

One of the most influential New Testament scholars of the twentieth century was Rudolf Bultmann, who came out of the Lutheran tradition. He studied theology at the universities of Tübingen, Berlin, and Marburg in Germany and taught at Marburg from 1921–51 when he retired. His first notable publication was *The History of the Synoptic Tradition,* which appeared in 1921. In this study he made use of a new scholarly tool, the form critical method, whereby he was able to separate the various layers of tradition observable in the Synoptic Gospels. Bultmann asserted that as a result of the available evidence, there is very little we can really know regarding the historical Jesus.[1]

It was Bultmann who raised again and again the question of the relevance of the message of Jesus to contemporary humanity. For him there is much that we would have to call mythological in the Gospels—requiring a "sacrifice of the intellect" to accept.

> His [Jesus'] person is viewed in the light of mythology when he is said to have been begotten of the Holy Spirit and born of the Virgin, and this becomes clearer still in the Hellenistic communities where he is understood to be the Son of God in a metaphysical sense.[2]

For Bultmann the message of the New Testament is formulated in the language of a primitive and prescientific mentality that has been described as mythological. According to this worldview, spirits from the other world are in combat with humankind, and all unusual happenings are brought about by these supernatural forces. The New Testament message has a mythological cast. Thus, in order for us to comprehend it, the message must be separated from its outmoded form.[3]

Bultmann suggests that we must look beyond such mythological notions and attend to other sayings of Jesus that are not problematic for contemporary humanity. His proclamation of the will of God, and his demands for sacrifice, love, and decision, we can accept with unquestioning hearts. But does this mean that we ignore entirely the mythological sayings and focus only on Christ's moral demands? No, this is not the answer. "We must ask whether the eschatological preaching and the mythological sayings as a whole contain a deeper meaning which is concealed under the cover of mythology."[4]

Mythology reveals a particular understanding of human life. According to this mentality, God is above and beyond the world and is in heaven. Hell is beneath the earth and is the seat of evil, ruled by Satan. Mythological eschatology, according to Bultmann, anticipates the end of the world, the judgment of God, and the beginning of the time of salvation or eternal punishment. For him these mythological conceptions have lost all meaning for modern humans and must be translated into the contemporary medium. The deeper meaning of the mythological preaching of Jesus is to be open to God's future because it is imminent for each of us. The moment of decision is at hand, and those who believe already possess eternal life. "To demythologize is to deny that the message of Scripture and of the Church is bound to an ancient world-view which is obsolete."[5] The thought patterns of modern humanity are formed by what can be called the scientific worldview. This scientific thinking, however, can tempt us to self-sufficiency, prompting us to forget that our lives will soon end in death. It is the Word of God that leads us away from our selfishness and a false sense of security, calling us to our true destiny.

> It is the Word of God which calls man to genuine freedom, into free obedience, and the task of demythologizing has no other purpose but to make clear the call of the Word of God. It will interpret the Scripture asking for the deeper meaning of mythological conceptions and freeing the Word of God from a by-gone world-view.[6]

Bultmann insists that there is little we can know about Jesus' life and personality from the New Testament. He is convinced that Jesus did not see himself as the Messiah. Rather, he was the eschatological prophet and could be considered a rabbi because of his teaching methods. He emphasized judgment, mercy, and fidelity. God leaves the particular decisions to the individual, as long as he or she realizes the need for decision in each moment of life. Christ taught the fatherhood of God, a teaching that was rather common among the Jews of his day. However, Bultmann affirms that neither Jesus nor the earliest Christians made any statements regarding his metaphysical nature. Rather, it was the Greek-speaking Christians who asserted that Jesus possesses a divine nature. As a matter of fact, only John 20:28 clearly speaks of Christ as God. According to Bultmann, several other New Testament passages refer to Jesus as divine (e.g., Titus 2:13), but their meaning is doubtful. The use of the word "Lord" or *kurios* identifies him as a divine figure, but not as God pure and simple. Through Jesus' words and actions God speaks to us and acts on our behalf. In him we encounter God in the most intense manner. However, Christ for Bultmann can best be described as the Word of God, and we should be satisfied with this.[7]

According to theologian John Macquarrie, Bultmann's notion of God is quite "elusive." He makes hardly any effort to conceptualize the divinity. "I have talked of his 'understanding' of God, but by this I do not mean an intellectual theory but a very existential type of understanding which is there only in that moment of experience when God touches a human life."[8] In Bultmann's *Jesus and the Word,* published in English in 1934, Macquarrie asserts that there are no direct affirmations concerning the nature of God.[9] We have God's Word that is addressed to us at a given moment, but very little else. We come to grips with the divine at the time when we are to make a decision in response to what we perceive as God's will for us. In that instance we are aware that the decision presenting itself to us will either take us toward the realization of our authentic selves or deflect us from it should we refuse to accept the initiative. Essentially, Bultmann's notion of God is focused on those moments when we are called upon to respond to the divine demand or invitation.[10] Macquarrie feels that Bultmann's concept of God is narrowly limited to our apprehension of the Deity in those individual moments of decision, foreclosing for us the possibility of an abiding and ever-deepening *ontological* understanding of God beyond and between those moments. This means that we have little opportunity to formulate in our minds a concept of God that we can hold on to, cherish, and deepen between the "moments of decision." Bultmann never seems to have gotten beyond this perception of God in his subsequent writings.

When Bultmann speaks about the kingdom of God, he is not referring to an event that will come to pass in the future. For him, whenever we humans are confronted with a critical decision, that particular hour is truly the ultimate hour.[11] Our worth is determined by the decisions we make in those important moments. The goal of these decisions is to act in accordance with the will of God, and we are assured that we will know what to do in these instances. Jesus did indeed predict the end of the age, and his demand for obedience is related to his awareness of the coming of the end time. Because of his concentration on that final time, Christ had little interest in the minute aspects of life in the world. The precise moral obligations related to our daily work, our familial relationships, or our civic duties were of little concern to Jesus because he sensed that the end was so close. He did not trouble himself setting out detailed directions for daily life because he perceived that ultimate closure was near at hand. Jesus was confident that his faithful followers would know what to do in their moments of decision. As the messianic prophet, he preached radical obedience to the will of God. In these instances we must decide for God and surrender our natural wills.[12] This "now" is what Bultmann calls the last hour.

Christ did not set out a detailed picture of the coming eschatological events. "He confined himself to the statement that the Kingdom of God will come and that men must be prepared to face the coming judgment."[13] Bultmann further affirms:

> Jesus envisaged the inauguration of the Kingdom of God as a tremendous cosmic drama. The Son of Man will come with the clouds of heaven, the dead will be raised and the day of judgment will arrive; and for the righteous the time of bliss will begin whereas the damned will be delivered to the torments of hell.[14]

It must be noted that Jesus' conception of the kingdom of God, as well as his idea of the eschatological drama, is indeed mythological. And Bultmann asks whether or not this notion of the kingdom of God has any currency for humanity today. Does Christ's eschatological preaching contain any message behind the myth, which has little value for our age? He insists that the message behind the myth is one of selfless love of neighbor upon which the judgment of God will be based.

The New Testament kerygma focuses on the proclamation of the decisive act of God in Christ. The mythological elements that have become a part of Christian eschatology are, for Bultmann, unbelievable to humankind come of age. They therefore are to be translated so as to preserve and emphasize the living character of the message. Bultmann's eschatological moment is really each individual's moment of ultimate decision before God. John Macquarrie sums up Bultmann's eschatological stance: "It may be noted that, like Barth, Bultmann seems to think of the eschaton much more in terms of judgment than of hope, and it seems questionable whether anywhere in his writings he gives clear expression to a hope beyond death."[15]

The late New Testament scholar Norman Perrin (1921-76) renders a similar verdict on Rudolf Bultmann's demythologizing. The eschatological images portrayed in the New Testament writings are to be interpreted in terms of our encountering God in the reality of our existence in the world.[16] God transformed the old world by making authentic existence possible. Perrin refers to the words of Bultmann:

> According to the New Testament, Jesus Christ is the eschatological event, the action of God by which God has set an end to the old world. In the preaching of the Christian Church the eschatological event will ever again become present and does become present ever and again in faith. . . . Jesus Christ is the eschatological event not as an established fact of past time but as repeatedly present, as addressing you and me here and now in preaching. Preaching is address, and as address it demands [an] answer, [a] decision.[17]

The future eschatological event described in Mark 13 as the end of the old world and the beginning of the new never occurred or ever will occur. "The action of God in the cross of Jesus and in the proclamation of that cross by the church is the eschatological event, by means of which 'God has set an end to the world.'"[18]

Oscar Cullmann (1902–99)

Baptized in the Lutheran communion and educated at the University of Strasbourg, Oscar Cullmann taught at the universities of Strasbourg, Basel, and Paris. He is recognized as one of the more prominent biblical scholars of the twentieth century. His important study *Christ and Time,* published in 1946, brought together the work of his previous ten years and articulated his view of redemptive history, which was quite different from the positions of Schweitzer and Bultmann. Cullmann's view of salvation opens with the event of the birth of Jesus and insists on a Christocentric view of history. His intention is to study the New Testament approach to time and history. He stresses the New Testament understanding of *kairos,* which he defines as a point in time especially favorable for a significant undertaking.[19] Jesus identified his future passion and death as his special *kairos* (Matt 26:18–29; John 7:6). Also, he sees the day of the Lord as the final *kairos,* which will come at a time that no one can anticipate (Mark 13:32). In Cullmann's judgment, eternity in the New Testament is not timelessness but rather an unlimited series of limited world periods whose successions are known only to God.[20]

The New Testament deals with a linear view of time. The passage of time is not circular, as with the Greeks, but linear, and it is consistently related to the redemptive process. For the early Christians, God was always seen and understood as being involved in the temporal process. The New Testament frequently alludes to two periods—the present age and the age of the eschaton. In Peter's speech as recorded in Acts 2:17ff., he describes the last days when God will pour out his Spirit on all flesh before the coming of the Lord's "great and glorious day" (v. 20). Cullmann observes that Paul's notion of *mysterion,* or mystery, is closely tied to the unfolding of the various stages of the redemptive process.

For Cullmann the midpoint of time is the Christ event, after which the end begins to draw near. For the first one or two Christian generations, the end was seen to be only a matter of decades away, but this presumption was corrected in the early second century (see 2 Pet 3:8–10). In fact, Paul modified his opinion regarding the proximity of the end from 1 Thessalonians 4:13–17 (ca. A.D. 50–51) to 2 Corinthians 5:1–10 (ca. A.D. 57). By the time of 2 Peter (ca. A.D. 120–130), a much longer interval—even beyond that envisioned by Paul—is assumed. Although Jesus himself before the high priest predicted his return in the imagery of Daniel 7:13 and Psalm 110, he offered no timeline (Mark 14:62). He did, however, expect an intermediate period after his death prior to the end time.[21] Cullmann affirms that the consistent eschatology of Albert Schweitzer, which insisted that eschatology was invariably the subject of primary importance among the early Christians, is overstated. It is evident that the first task of the church in the early centuries was the promulgation of the gospel, which must take place before the end (Mark 13:30–33). According to Matthew, the end of days will come only after the gospel has been preached to all people (24:14). All must be given an opportunity to hear the good news.[22]

Cullmann affirms that the early church formulated the New Testament canon around A.D. 150 in order to submit to its control all further traditions, thus asserting its view that henceforth all subsequent traditions are to be subjected to the canonical Scriptures. From A.D. 150 the apostolic age was thus viewed as the foundational period of the church. "The Ancient Church created the New Testament canon when it became clear that the Church was continuing while the apostles were all dead, and precisely in this fixing of the apostolic witness it remained true to the original evaluation of the apostolate as a unique function."[23] Cullmann affirms that Matthew 16:18 is not to be seen as a justification for a continuing papal office in the church. The saying, "You are Peter . . ." is addressed to this apostle and to him alone inasmuch as he is the "once-for-all" established foundation of the church. The foundation of a house is laid but once at the beginning.[24]

All salvation is to come through Christ, who after the ascension sits at the right hand of God, and all things are gathered up in him (Eph 1:10). Christ has reconciled with himself everything that is on earth and in heaven. According to Ephesians 1:1–4, every person is elected or chosen as an individual. Justification is essentially the application of the redemptive process to the individual. Cullmann declares that the continuation of the life of the soul after death is not the result of a natural process. Indeed, a divine intervention is required if there is to be a resurrection.[25] The biblical view of life beyond death—contrary to the Greek philosophers' understanding of the immortality of the human soul—must involve the resurrection of the body. Further, in the Christian perspective, every resurrection must be derived from the resurrection of Christ, whose risen and glorified body exists now. The Holy Spirit is the power through whom God has brought about the resurrection of Jesus (Rom 1:4).

The transformation of our earthly bodies into spiritual bodies is to occur on the final day. "The New Testament knows nothing of an immediate resurrection of the body that will occur for each one immediately after death. . . . To be sure, the believer already has eternal life, but here too the raising of the body takes place only on the last day."[26] The New Testament assures us that those who die in Christ are with him immediately after death (Luke 23:43), but the bodily resurrection is reserved for the end time. Paul urges us to be confident that the just will be with Christ even before their bodies are raised. Indeed, we will have the Spirit as our assurance and our pledge that we will soon be clothed with our "heavenly dwelling" (2 Cor 5:1–10). "[T]he being with Christ does not yet signify resurrection of the body, but does signify a closer connection with Christ which is already affected through the resurrection power of the Holy Spirit."[27] The dead who die in Christ will await the moment when they will be clothed with a spiritual body. This intermediate state is not described in the New Testament, and for Cullmann, an excessive interest in the details is a demonstration of little faith. He has no interest in the doctrine of purgatory.

Based on a series of lectures delivered at Harvard in 1954–55, Cullmann published a small volume titled *Immortality of the Soul or Resurrection of the Dead?* in 1958.[28] This study expands somewhat the author's observations set out in *Christ and Time*. He claims that the early Christians believed that the human soul is not naturally immortal but only becomes immortal through faith in the resurrection of Christ.[29] The Greeks taught that the body is unworthy of the human soul and must be destroyed in order to free the soul. This teaching is unacceptable to Christian belief. According to the teaching of the New Testament, humans who die in Christ are recalled to life by virtue of a new divine act of creation. This anthropology is related more to Jewish thought. For Paul both the body and the soul are divine creations that were originally good, but human sin has defiled them. Through the salvation of Christ, both soul and body can experience resurrection. Not only will faith in the resurrection of Jesus make our souls immortal, but the Spirit will one day quicken, restore, and spiritualize our mortal bodies (Rom 8:11). Cullmann insists that because of passages such as Matthew 10:28, the human soul is not by nature immortal. Therefore, there must be a resurrection for both the soul and the body. The resurrection of the body, however, will not occur until the last day.[30] Christ is the firstborn from the dead. His risen body is the first spiritual body. All the faithful must patiently await that day when they will receive their spiritual bodies in a new act of creation.

All of us live in the interim period between Christ's bodily resurrection and our own. Our "inner man" is already undergoing transformation through the efforts of the Holy Spirit (2 Cor 4:16). Cullmann does not agree with Barth that the transformation of the body occurs for all immediately after death. Those who die in Christ are waiting for that moment. They do, however, enjoy a special closeness to God, and they participate in the tension of the interim period. For Paul they are asleep.[31] The intermediate state is that period during which the soul—after its resurrection but before it receives its spiritual body—exists with the Holy Spirit who continues to transform and perfect the soul.

The fact that even in this state the dead are already living with Christ does not correspond to the natural essence of the soul. Rather it is the result of a divine intervention from the outside, through the Holy Spirit, who must have already quickened the inner man in earthly life by his miraculous power.[32]

The transformation of the body will also be accomplished by the Holy Spirit at the appointed time. Cullmann concludes that the hope of resurrection reflected in the New Testament is very different from the belief in immortality as taught by Socrates and Plato.

Nearly twenty years after the writing of *Christ and Time,* Cullmann published *Salvation in History,* written in appreciation for his having been invited to take part in the sessions of Vatican II (1962–65).[33] Once again he addresses the position of Rudolf Bultmann, who opposed the notion of an evolving salvation history. For Albert Schweitzer, when Jesus sent out his disciples to proclaim the gospel to the lost sheep of the house of Israel (Matt 10:5–7), he anticipated that the end would come soon. When the disciples returned from their mission and the end had not come, Jesus announced that his own death would be the date of the coming of the end time.[34]

Bultmann's view, however, was not at all concerned with affirming an interim between the life of Jesus and the end of days. His eschatology was solely oriented to the contemporary situations of decision. In an effort to make the gospel relevant to humankind today, Bultmann removes the passage of time from the eschatological equation. The crucial moment is the present moment of decision, thus divesting eschatology of its thrust toward the future. He insists that the assumption of a "salvation history" alluded to in Luke and Acts was the product of "early catholicism." The flow of salvific events for Bultmann is not important. The only critical matter is our individual encounter with these events and our response to their call for decision.

For Cullmann, salvation history, which Paul termed the divine mystery, involves a series of events that are connected, with one leading to the other. Bultmann, on the other hand, had little time for salvation history. For him it is our decision in the moment of encounter with the wholly other that alone matters. The tension, however, between the already and the not yet is deeply embedded in the fabric of the New Testament. Jesus proclaimed that the end was coming within the generation of his contemporaries, although the day and the hour were unknown (Mark 9:1; 13:32). The later New Testament writings anticipated a longer period of time between Christ's ascension and his second coming, and the specific mission during this critical period is the preaching of the gospel. The early conviction of an imminent end gradually disappeared (2 Pet 3:8–9). The notion that Jesus assumed a continuation of the interval after his death and before the end time can, in Cullmann's judgment, hardly be doubted.[35]

The sweep of salvation history is dramatically illustrated in the parable of the wicked tenants (Mark 12:1–12). When the owner of the vineyard sent out a number of his servants to collect the rent from the tenants of the vineyard, each of the servants was treated with disdain. The owner then sent his own son, whom the wicked tenants tortured and killed. This parable reveals the historical dimension of the salvation of God that was brought to the Jews through the Old Testament prophets, and finally through his son. All of these messengers were ignored and rebuffed by the Jews. In Matthew 10:5 Jesus instructed the disciples to restrict their missionary activity to Israel alone. However, in Christ's discussion with a certain centurion in Capernaum, he foretold that many will come from the East and from the West to eat with Abraham, Isaac, and Jacob in the heavenly kingdom, while many of the original heirs of the kingdom will be left in darkness (Matt 8:11–12).

Cullmann continues to insist on the historical dimension of the salvation proclaimed and promised by the Old Testament prophets and fully revealed by Christ. He emphasizes that salvation history was deeply embedded in the self-consciousness of Jesus. Moreover, Christ's declaration before the high priest in Mark 14:62 is seen by Cullmann as a formal declaration by Christ that there would be an interval before his second coming.

Paul Tillich (1886–1965)

Paul Tillich's masterpiece *Systematic Theology* was published over a period of some twelve years. Volume 1, *Reason and Revelation: Being and God,* appeared in 1951 when Tillich was teaching at Union Theological in New York. Volume 2, *Existence and the Christ,* was completed in 1957 when he was a professor at Harvard. And volume 3, *Life and the Spirit: History and the Kingdom of God,* was issued in 1963 while he was teaching at the University of Chicago.[36] Before coming to the United States in 1933, Tillich taught at several German universities including Berlin and Marburg before he was dismissed from his university chair and left Germany in 1933 because of his antagonism against Hitler's national socialism. Tillich was also an extremely effective preacher whose collections of sermons can be considered outstanding contributions in themselves. Two of the most popular are *The Shaking of the Foundations* and *The New Being*.[37] His *Dynamics of Faith* is considered to be the best popular summary of his theology.[38]

Tillich's eschatology is to be found in the third volume of his *Systematic Theology*, in the section "History and the Kingdom of God." Because eschatology deals with the relation of the temporal to the eternal, one can begin one's treatment of systematic theology with the eschatological question, for it focuses on the "inner aim" of everything that is.[39] Tillich identifies the churches as the representatives of the kingdom of God in history. Within the churches lives what he calls the Spiritual Community. "[T]he church, the Spiritual Community, *always* lives in the churches and that where there are churches confessing their foundations in the Christ as the central manifestation of the Kingdom of God in history, there the church is,"[40] Moreover, the churches—since they represent the kingdom of God in history—are unable to forfeit this role even if they are sending a message that is in partial conflict with the message of the kingdom. One of the principal tasks of the churches is to continue to emphasize the tension between the awareness of the present and the anticipation of the final day, for this current stage of history will one day surely come to an end.

For Tillich, eschatology can be described as a study of those events that will occur in the last of all days. He insists that the study of the last days must never be considered an appendix to preaching and theology. Whether and how individuals might enter the realm of the transcendent is, for Tillich, the key challenge of human existence. As life moves toward its end, the positive elements in existence are elevated into eternal life, which is none other than a participation in the divine life. This transformation involves the freeing of the positive from its admixture with the negative elements. What masquerades as positive, but is really not, is cast aside. For God everything that is positive is a part of being itself and can never be discarded. Tillich affirms that everything that is, insofar as it is, is to be included in eternity. However, the good that still contains a mixture of nonbeing or evil must wait until the nonbeing is removed before it enters eternity. The negative or the nonbeing will be eliminated and will not be remembered. It is carried in the eternal memory as that which is thrown into nothingness. This is the negative dimension of what Tillich terms the ultimate or last judgment.

The saving side of the ultimate judgment involves the taking up into eternity of what a being essentially is. This process is called essentialization (Friedrich Schelling's term), which means that what has been actualized in time contributes something positive to essential being and in this manner produces what Tillich calls the "New Being." "Participation in the eternal life depends on a creative synthesis of a being's essential nature with what it has made of itself in its temporal existence."[41] Eternal life involves the finalizing of self-integration, self-creativity, and self-transcendence. Thus, for example, a person pushes beyond himself or herself toward the full realization of his or her ultimate destiny. "In eternal life the center of the individual person rests in the all-uniting divine center and through it in communion with all the personal centers."[42]

Tillich terms the divine life the definitive conquest of the negative. At the same time it is by no means a state of immobility. Rather, the divine life continues to evolve and to increase. God is ever going out from Godself to overcome the negativities of life. Everything that is will participate in the divine life of blessedness, and thus there will be "a new heaven and a new earth" in God's final kingdom. Tillich cites one of his favorite New Testament passages in describing the final blessedness of the universe: "The creation itself will be set free from its bondage to decay and will obtain the freedom of the glory of the children of God" (Rom 8:21).

The destiny of the individual is the next object of Paul Tillich's concern. The lot of the individual human being is determined by the decisions the person makes in life, and these are to a considerable extent determined by the potentialities bestowed on the individual. Tillich prefers the notion of essentialization as the appropriate description of what happens in human life because it allows for the loss of wasted potentialities and the regret connected with that loss. At the same time, this process insures the elevation and completion of what is positive in human existence into eternal blessedness. He does not accept, however, the theory of double predestination whereby some are destined for blessedness and others for endless punishment. Tillich feels that this theory places what he calls an eternal split into the Godhead.[43] To the extent that something *is*, it is included in the eternal blessedness. No human being is clearly and certainly on one side or the other of God's judgment. The social and environmental conditions into which we are born and in which we live our lives influence to a considerable extent how we grow, develop, and make our decisions. Further, the way in which we interpret and understand what Tillich calls the distorted forms of life, for example, the death of infants, and those afflicted with biological and psychological diseases of one sort or another, is simply beyond our power to comprehend.

Immortality must eventually be redefined, according to Tillich, for the concept of continued life without a body must be radically revised by Christianity. The early Christian theologians had recourse to Plato and the Neo-Platonists and took over the concept of the immortal soul as the foundation for all their thinking regarding life after death. The apostle Paul in 1 Corinthians 15:42ff. speaks of the physical body being raised up as a spiritual body; what is perishable becomes imperishable. This perishable body of ours must put on imperishability, and this mortal body is to put on immortality. Our finite corporeality is to be taken up and transformed into the eternal. The Spirit, in Paul's judgment comes into the human spirit, elevating and transforming it.

According to Tillich, the strong Christian emphasis on the resurrection of the body emphasizes the critical importance of each individual's uniqueness and irreplaceability. For Tillich it is imperative that the self-conscious self not be excluded from eternal life. It cannot be denied eternal fulfillment, just as the bodily dimension of humanity cannot be excluded from the eternal blessedness. Moreover, the self-conscious self in eternity will not merely enjoy the endless continuation of its customary stream of consciousness, but will experience a consciousness that goes on expanding, and that is ever new. The notion of resurrection is an ideal symbol for expressing Tillich's foundational concept of the New Being. "As the New Being is not another being, but the transformation of the old being, so resurrection is not the creation of another reality over against the old reality, but is the transformation of the old reality arising out of its death."[44]

Paul Tillich has great difficulty with the notion of eternal death that has been so prominent in the traditional preaching and teaching of the churches. It seems to run contrary to the truth that every created being is rooted in the eternal ground of being, and hence nonbeing cannot overcome it. "How can we reconcile the seriousness of the threat of death *away* from eternal life with the truth that everything comes from eternity and must return to it?"[45] The prospect of eternal death, which has been so much a part of the teaching of the churches, does run counter to the thesis of the universal restoration of all professed by Origen and others. This thesis of *apokatástasis pantōn* (universal restoration) has been generally feared by the mainstream Christian churches as compromising the critical importance of ethical decision making on the part of individuals. Do not human decisions have a lasting import, or are they simply washed away with the passage of time? Tillich insists that the theses of eternal death and of universal restoration are unacceptable. To overcome this dilemma, great numbers—especially in Asia—have embraced the theory of reincarnation, but this seems to dilute and destroy the individual's identity in and through the several incarnations. The Catholic concept of purgatory is problematic for Tillich because he feels that uninterrupted periods of nothing but suffering are impossible to imagine. He affirms that Protestantism abolished the doctrine because of the many abuses that it brought in its wake.

The doctrine of predestination never appealed to Tillich because it builds on the assumption that God does not love or care for great numbers of human beings. This is directly opposed to the prevailing notion that God created the world and all that is in it out of love and earnestly wills the realization of all created potentialities. The symbols of heaven and hell are really grounded in the degrees of fulfillment or nonfulfillment that individuals are able and willing to achieve during their lifetimes as they move toward their essentialization in eternal life.[46] These symbols provide a certain perspective for persons as they advance toward their final destiny—to shun the danger of eternal death and to embrace the promise of eternal life.

Eternal life can be defined as life in God. According to the apostle Paul, ultimate fulfillment consists in God's being all in all, which for Tillich means the radical essentialization of all created reality, especially of all humans. The basic rhythm of life in our earthly context passes through self-realization, estrangement, and reconciliation, which is really the movement through existence to essentialization that is achieved in eternity. Everything that has being is prompted by God toward the full actualization of its potentialities and its ultimate essentialization.

A word must be added regarding Tillich's sermons. Through his simple yet elegant homilies, Tillich has drawn a portrait of his theology, which in a nontechnical manner introduces his seminal concepts such as essentialization, ultimate concern, and the New Being. In his own fashion he charts his understanding of the way to "the new heaven and the new earth."

Observations

Rudolf Bultmann, Oscar Cullmann, and Paul Tillich are important in that they reach out to the very parameters of the eschatological question as well as any twentieth-century theologians. Bultmann and Cullmann are two premier biblical theologians, while Tillich is a systematic theologian of the first rank. These three Protestant scholars lay out the state of the question and set the stage for further discussion.

NOTES

1. Roger Johnson, *Rudolf Bultmann: Interpreting Faith for the Modern Era* (San Francisco: Collins, 1987), 9–11.

2. Rudolf Bultmann, *Jesus Christ and Mythology* (New York: Scribner's, 1958), 16–17.

3. Van A. Harvey, *A Handbook of Theological Terms* (New York: Macmillan, 1964), 67–68, 155–56.

4. Bultmann, *Jesus Christ and Mythology*, 18.

5. Ibid., 36.

6. Ibid., 43.

7. William La Due, *Jesus among the Theologians: Contemporary Interpretations of Christ* (Harrisburg, Pa.: Trinity Press International, 2001), 59–62.

8. John Macquarrie, *Thinking about God* (London: SCM Press, 1975), 179.

9. Ibid., 181.

10. Ibid., 187.

11. Rudolf Bultmann, *Jesus and the Word* (trans. Louise Smith and Erminie Lantero; New York: Scribner's, 1958), 52.

12. Ibid., 131.

13. Bultmann, *Jesus Christ and Mythology*, 12.

14. Ibid., 13.

15. Macquarrie, *Thinking about God*, 100–101.

16. Norman Perrin, *The Promise of Bultmann* (New York: J. B. Lippincott, 1969), 45–46.

17. Rudolf Bultmann, *History and Eschatology: The Presence of Eternity* (New York: Harper & Row, 1957), 151–52.

18. Perrin, *Promise of Bultmann*, 46.

19. Oscar Cullmann, *Christ and Time* (trans. Floyd F. Filson; London: SCM Press, 1951; rev. ed. 1962), 39.

20. Ibid., 46.

21. Ibid., 149.

22. Ibid., 163.

23. Ibid., 172.

24. Ibid., 173.

25. Ibid., 234.

26. Ibid., 237–38.

27. Ibid., 240.

28. Oscar Cullmann, *Immortality of the Soul or Resurrection of the Dead? The Witness of the New Testament* (London: Epworth Press, 1958).

29. Ibid., 17.
30. Ibid., 37.
31. Ibid., 51.
32. Ibid., 56.
33. Oscar Cullmann, *Salvation in History* (trans. Sidney G. Sowers; New York: Harper & Row, 1967).
34. Ibid., 30.
35. Ibid., 226.
36. Paul Tillich, *Systematic Theology* (3 vols. in 1; Chicago: University of Chicago Press, 1967).
37. Paul Tillich, *The Shaking of the Foundations* (New York: Scribner's, 1948); *The New Being* (New York: Scribner's, 1955).
38. Paul Tillich, *Dynamics of Faith* (New York: Harper & Row, 1957).
39. Tillich, *Systematic Theology,* vol. 3, 298.
40. Ibid., 378.
41. Ibid., 401.
42. Ibid., 402.
43. Ibid., 407.
44. Ibid., 414.
45. Ibid., 415.
46. Ibid., 418.

3

RAHNER, BOROS, AND RATZINGER: TRADITIONAL TWENTIETH-CENTURY CATHOLIC PRESENTATIONS OF ESCHATOLOGY

Karl Rahner (1904–84)

Widely recognized as the outstanding Catholic theologian of the twentieth century, Karl Rahner did his graduate studies at Freiburg in Germany and Innsbruck in Austria. After World War II he returned to the University of Innsbruck as a professor of theology. From 1964 to 1967 he taught at the University of Munich, and from 1967 to his retirement in 1971, he taught at the University of Münster. His many articles on a whole range of theological subjects were collected over the years and published in the series *Theological Investigations,* which comes to some twenty-three volumes in English. This collection was issued from the early 1960s to the early 1990s. Although his other writings are too numerous to chronicle here, one of his latest works, *Foundations of Christian Faith,* which appeared in English in 1978, represents perhaps the most valuable summary of his theology. Toward the end of his life, he said, "[W]hat is most important [among his theological writings] is contained more or less in my *Foundations of Christian Faith.*"[1]

One of his more influential early studies on the subject of eschatology, *On the Theology of Death,* appeared in English in 1961. Rahner insists that death marks the absolute end of our state of pilgrimage, after which our eternal lot will be definitively determined. Each individual's free self-affirmation is achieved once and for all in death. He asserts that our lives are permeated by the prospect of death. The traditional description of death as the separation of the soul from the body is not to be found in the Scriptures. He asks whether the soul leaves the world when a person dies or whether it enters into some sort of cosmic relationship with the world. Perhaps the soul, no longer bound to an individual body, assumes a deeper linkage with the universe itself. Rahner affirms that the soul possesses a transcendental relationship with matter that continues after death. He speculates that "it becomes permissible to suppose . . . that the human spiritual soul will, in some way or other, maintain her relationship with the world."[2]

This does not imply that the soul is present everywhere in the universe, but it is conceivable that it in some fashion becomes a codetermining force in the cosmos. Thus, in death, the human soul's relationship to the universe is transformed into what Rahner terms a world-embracing relationship, which is no longer channeled through one's body. Although in death one attains his or her final determination and destiny, the human soul experiences disharmony with the world and makes every effort to be reconciled after death with the right order of things. This is the point of departure for Rahner's view of purgatory.

Although we have not yet discovered the natural grounds for the necessity of death, Rahner teaches that humankind was created with the possibility of immunity from death. However, the human race has fallen away from God, and that has changed everything. Had sin not entered the world, Adam would have possibly experienced an end to his life in another manner, without having to undergo the rigors of death. It was difficult indeed for Rahner to reconcile the notion of death as a natural phenomenon that all must experience in some fashion, with the idea of death as guilt resulting from human sinfulness. Death amounts to the transformation of the human being into the state of a free spirit. However, Rahner does not explain precisely what he intends by this change. Can this mean that we are absorbed into some sort of universal spirit, or do we still retain our individual and distinct mode of existence?[3] He leaves this question open for further deliberation.

The articles of the Christian creed remind us that after his death, Christ visited the limbo of the Fathers, although no reference to this event can be found in the New Testament. Rahner wants us to think of Christ as making a connection here with the deepest level of the world, thus becoming an intrinsic principle of the world's transformation. "When the vessel of his body was shattered in death, Christ was poured out over all the world; he became actually in his humanity, what he had always been according to his dignity, the heart of the world, the innermost center of creation."[4] Rahner offers this view as a possible interpretation of the death of Jesus.

It is only in death that we become integrated into the universe. Our spiritual reality becomes part of the world and expands the permanent destiny of the universe. We must consider the act of dying as an eminently human act that gathers up the whole of one's existence into one final consummation.[5] Our confidence must be grounded in the fact that "everyone who lives and believes in me [Jesus] will never die" (John 11:26).

In his study "The Resurrection of the Body," which appeared in volume 2 of *Theological Investigations,* Karl Rahner attacks those who sneer at the resurrection of the body.[6] These Christian demythologizers are flying in the face of the declarations of every catechism and creed. It must be affirmed, however, that this article of faith has had a rather troubled existence. During the Middle Ages concentration came to be focused on the soul's direct vision of God in the afterlife. After Pope Benedict XII declared in 1336 that the souls of the just enjoy the direct vision of God soon after death, attention was shifted somewhat from the bodily resurrection to the soul's experience in the life beyond. Rahner asks what we really mean by the resurrection of the body and then proposes that it refers to the whole human person with his or her embodied reality, constituting the perfection of the whole individual, present before God and sharing eternal life.[7]

After death, the person remains somehow united with the reality of the world, although this concept is not easy to imagine. We shall always be a part of the world's destiny as it moves toward its own ultimate fulfillment. Rahner attests that Christ's second coming will occur when our world reaches its final transformation. Although it is difficult to envision, our bodily resurrection is to be a part of this ultimate transformation of the cosmos. By reflection on the experience of the risen Christ as reported in the New Testament, we can grasp some idea of the condition of bodies after the final resurrection. Paul assures us that the risen body will be a spiritual body (1 Cor 15:42–44) that is animated by the Spirit of God. Rahner speculates that since the risen person has a spatial determination of some sort, we are inclined to envision heaven as a place rather than merely a state.[8] This final condition is not to be portrayed as a heaven of pure spirits, for this view fails to do justice to the reality of humankind as children of the earth.

> Whoever does not believe that both of them [matter and spirit], once reconciled, can come to the one completion, denies in the last analysis that the one God has created matter and spirit in one act for one end. . . . The belief for this solution and the courage for such a solution he [the Christian] draws from the Word of God alone. But God's Word testifies to the resurrection of the body.[9]

In an extended monograph that appears in volume 4 of *Theological Investigations*, "The Hermeneutics of Eschatological Assertions," Rahner investigates the value of eschatological statements and how to interpret them in our day. He alleges that this question has been treated more adequately in the writings of Protestant theologians.[10] Once again he takes issue with Bultmann and the demythologizers who say that eschatological statements in Scripture refer exclusively to things that take place here and now. Rahner retorts that the preaching of the church from the earliest days intended to make assertions about the future. Thus, the position of Bultmann and his followers is theologically unacceptable. We cannot arbitrarily establish limits beyond which God cannot or may not reveal future occurrences. If the Godhead wishes to disclose to humans certain future events, this is certainly within the capacity of Godself. And if these disclosures are veiled in obscure language for whatever reason, this is well within the province of God. Furthermore, we should not read the eschatological assertions of Scripture with an eye to reconstructing as precisely as possible the future event that is portrayed.

Rahner also reminds his readers that if the virtues of faith and hope are to have any real meaning, the saving events of the future must be hidden to us. "It is essential that the eschatological be hidden in its revelation."[11] Eschatology is vital because it offers a view of the future that humans require for making decisions that are grounded in their freedom and their faith. The pictures and images afforded by the Scriptures regarding the events of the end time are difficult to reconcile and harmonize, but they do clearly point us to the future and leave us with a sense of mystery regarding the final days. Rahner emphasizes that eschatology moves from the present to the future, while apocalyptic, which is usually based on fantasy, starts from the future and works back to the present.

The possibility of ultimate salvation or loss must always be left open to humans, and therefore the prospect of a universal restoration (i.e., the eventual salvation of all) must not be included in our hopes for the future. The possibility of damnation must be left open, since it is forbidden to humans before death to be certain of their ultimate triumph.[12] In Rahner's judgment, the intermediate state (purgatory) must be regarded as a dogma with a credible biblical foundation. The doctrine of purgatory accounts for the fact that many facets of our personhood do not usually attain perfection at the same time, and therefore a full maturation of the whole person after death is called for prior to the individual's entrance into glory. In the particular judgment,

God's final decision is directed toward each individual, while the general judgment will look to the progress of humankind as a whole and to the shape and dimensions of the final victory of God.

In his later study, *Foundations of Christian Faith,* Rahner reaffirms that both the Old and New Testaments reveal a great deal about the future.[13] Eschatological statements project into the future our graced experiences in the present, although the images of the last days remain for us quite mysterious. We must, however, in our hopes for the future, remain fast in our conviction concerning the absolute unity of matter and spirit. "Christian anthropology would be false if it wanted to ascribe immortality only to the soul and make its destiny independent of the transformation of the world."[14]

Rahner then sets out his views regarding individual eschatology. Although the cosmic plan of salvation history will indeed reach a positive outcome through the grace of God, we cannot be certain of the final destiny of individuals who could conceivably lose their way. He reaffirms that the doctrine of *apokatástasis,* asserting the salvation of absolutely everyone, is not a tenable position. Yet at the same time we cannot say of any human being who has ever lived that he or she is certainly lost. Further, Rahner feels that it is pointless to speculate on the status and mode of existence of individuals while their bodies are in the grave and their souls are already with God. The reality of the human being in death takes on a new type of life. Rahner reminds us that we certainly do not continue on after death as though we only change horses and ride on (Feuerbach).[15] In death we are transformed into a new sort of existence, which is not merely a continuation of our temporal life beyond the portal of death.

The definitive evaluation of human life is realized at the moment of death. After that point there is no essential change in one's ultimate destiny. Rahner describes eternity as one's entrance into God's presence either with an absolute decision of love for the Deity or with an irrevocable decision that eternally closes one off from God. In the Scriptures we find that no human life is portrayed as so unimportant or common that it would not be valuable enough to live on into eternity. The life of the blessed after death is portrayed as peace and rest, as a banquet, as being at home in the Father's house, and as the endless joy of communion with God and the friends of God.

Although Rahner concedes that the doctrine of purgatory is not generally accepted by Protestant believers, he insists that because the complex process of human maturation is not realized in every area of human existence all at once, there are phases in the human growth process that call for a time after death when all the various elements of human behavior can catch up to one's radical decision for God. However, he readily admits that much needs to be explored in this critical area of theology.

In addition to the eternal destiny of the individual, there is a cosmic eschatology that requires attention. The world will not simply continue on forever, for it too approaches its final destiny, which will spell out the end of history. We must not fall into a purely existential interpretation that focuses only on individuals and their destiny, for the cosmos is also approaching the time of its fulfillment. This will be a graced event that the New Testament has foretold and anticipated. The discipline of eschatology has regrettably for too long concentrated on the future of individuals, giving little attention to the cosmic dimension. Perhaps this era is coming to an end and the age of cosmic eschatology will now become much more important. Although the New Testament data is rich and inviting, the development of this other half of the discipline has been largely neglected.

Rahner observes that the study of eschatology has not advanced beyond a relatively superficial arrangement of the data found in the Scriptures.[16] Even the basic terms of eschatology have not as yet received sufficient treatment and analysis. For example, we have only begun to evaluate theologically the world in its process of becoming. Also, we must account for the possibility of extending the habitation of humans beyond the limits of this earth. The Scriptures have had recourse to a number of models that are challenging and in some cases relatively impossible to reconcile. For example, in one scenario the final end is portrayed as a world conflagration, and in another as a vast judgment scene wherein all of humankind is assembled together. We profess that the resurrection of the body is a tenet of faith, yet we are unable to envision how this resurrection will come about. Nor is it likely that we are able to coordinate in a fully convincing fashion the biblical imagery of individual and cosmic eschatology.

Rahner reminds his readers that there is still much to clarify concerning the relationship between heaven and what he calls "the reprobate world." Also, a deeper understanding of the so-called intermediate state between death and the general judgment must be pursued by theologians and biblicists, for the New Testament and the early Christian traditions are relatively rich in unexplored data. Although we are beginning to investigate the dimensions of universal eschatology and its promise of "a new heaven and a new earth," this field is vast indeed. There is much work to be done regarding such issues as the final return of Christ, the resurrection of the flesh, and the ultimate transfiguration of the world. Also, the precise relationship between the particular judgment soon after our death and the general judgment at the end of time continues to remain mysterious.

In an interview on the occasion of his seventy-fifth birthday, Rahner made specific reference to a subject that concerned him deeply:

> One or two years ago, I really had the intention of writing something about a possible orthodox teaching on *apokatástasis*, the doctrine that all free beings will eventually share in the grace of salvation. . . . Despite certain texts in the New Testament I do not know with absolute certainty that eternal loss occurs for any particular people. . . . So I would still really like to have written something about such a teaching on *apokatástasis* that would be orthodox and acceptable.[17]

Ladislaus Boros (1927–)

Born in Budapest and educated at various Jesuit scholasticates and at the University of Munich, Ladislaus Boros taught the philosophy of religion for some years at the University of Innsbruck. His most important study, *The Mystery of Death,* was published in English in 1965.[18] His interpretation of the so-called "final option" has aroused much discussion since the appearance of his work almost forty years ago.

Boros sketches a portrait of death as he envisions it. He lays out his thesis as follows:

> Death gives man the opportunity of posing his first completely personal act; death is, therefore, by reason of its very being, the moment above all others for the awakening of consciousness, for freedom, for the encounter with God, for the final decision about his eternal destiny.[19]

A philosophical investigation precedes Boros's theological treatment of the subject. The linchpin of his entire presentation is the notion of death as the unique and privileged moment when a person has the capacity to make a full and definitive decision for or against God. The final decision that the individual makes in this regard cannot be made before death or after death, but only *in* death. It is in the moment of death, as the soul departs from the body, that the soul becomes fully awake and fully capable of grasping the whole expanse of its being in one single irrevocable act.

During our lives we are confronted daily with the mystery of our existence. Boros is convinced that we are incapable of fully entering into our own acts and are thus unable, during life, to become persons in the full sense. We feel uncertain even in the everyday corners of our lives and often have a sense that we are not really at home among familiar things. At times we experience that we do not belong, and an unremitting restlessness colors everything we do. Our whole life is crowded with unfulfilled goals and expectations. We always expect more of our lives yet seldom seem to attain our objectives. For Boros, only in death will the human soul possess a wholly genuine opportunity for making its fully personal decision.[20]

Humans never seem to be able to avoid "ever wanting more." We are constantly pushed by the momentum of our being to search for more, because what we have already acquired never seems to satisfy us. "Only in the act of our meeting with God can we catch up with ourselves and really become human beings. . . . If, however, God can never be overtaken in this life, then it is equally true that our deepest self can never be overtaken by us."[21] At some point, insists Boros, our unconscious drive toward God and our movement toward conscious self-realization must coincide. We are not capable of positing the total direction of our lives during our lifetime, but only in death can we accomplish the full positing of our freedom. Also, our intellect, in its knowledge of limited being, is actually reaching out to the absolute expanse of being, the infinite reality of God. Our first total act of knowing is possible only at the moment of death when the mind is freed from the body. In death we become capable of our first fully personal act. Death provides the occasion for what Boros calls "total intuition," when the human person comes into the possession of his or her undivided life. Then and only then can the individual make the full and integral decision concerning the final disposition of one's existence.

Boros claims that in our youth we are filled with vitality in the pursuit of various goals, but this vitality gradually wanes and we realize all that we could have been. As the world begins to slip away from us, we withdraw into our inner selves. We abandon our illusions of success and achievement and retire within. This inner person who develops can, according to Boros, only fully emerge in death. "In death man becomes for the first time and finally, a person, an independent and spiritualized center of being."[22] In the process of death the human soul is actually brought into greater proximity to the material world. It does not become "acosmic" but enters into a deeper relationship with matter and becomes "pancosmic." In death the soul moves toward the heart of the universe, and there it will make its "complete and final decision." This decision at this juncture lasts forever. "Death is a man's first completely personal act, and is therefore, by reason of its very being, the place above all others for the awakening of consciousness, for freedom, for the encounter with God, for the final decision about eternal destiny."[23]

After Boros concludes the philosophical treatment of his thesis, he proceeds to add a theological dimension. He reaffirms that death certainly closes our options regarding our final destiny, and he insists that such a definitive determination of our eternal future calls for the full possession of our faculties "in complete lucidity and freedom." This full awareness and full volition, according to Boros, are only available to us at the time of death. However, this hypothesis of a final decision does not destroy in any way the value of the decisions made during our lives, such that we would have to look upon them as relatively meaningless. "It does indeed offer the possibility of correcting at the end all the decisions of a whole lifetime, but the complete re-directing of a whole life's fundamental orientation must always be looked on as an extreme case in the order of probability."[24]

The final decision, although connected with our total life's course, does stand above all the decisions we have made during our lives, and it renders our conclusive and definitive judgment on them. There is little likelihood that we will reverse our life course at the time of death, but Boros holds out this possibility. He makes it clear, however, that this final option does not imply that all will choose God. People can decide against God even when they are completely aware of what they are doing in full freedom. In death each person has "the possibility of making a fully personal choice for or against God."[25] Boros takes a negative stand on the limbo hypothesis, which has enjoyed only limited favor in recent times. According to his theory of a final decision, infants would surely be able to make the choice for or against God with full knowledge and freedom at the time of their death. Also, for Boros, had Adam not sinned, he and the rest of the human family would not have had to undergo the disintegration of their bodies in death but would have passed immediately into a resurrected state without having to abandon their bodies.[26]

The question of purgatory in his judgment need not be envisioned as a place but rather as a process, a momentary process that is experienced as a personal encounter with God after death. As the individual turns toward God, there is a cleansing that involves pain, wherein the love of God penetrates into the many layers of our consciousness and purifies us through and through. The degree of pain is commensurate with the level of cleansing that is called for in each case.

The importance of the hypothesis of a final option is also valuable in demonstrating that Christ's death was really what effectively redeemed humankind. Although some theologians have maintained that any action of Jesus could have saved the world, the hypothesis of a final decision at the moment of death would better explain his descent into the lower regions of the earth, which grounded a new relationship between him and all of humanity. We now can meet Christ everywhere. "The whole evolving cosmos is a transparency of Christ, which is why we can discover Christ at the heart of all things and happenings with his reality as God-man."[27] Christ's resurrection and ascension constitute the completion of the universal presence of Christ in the cosmos.

Boros concludes that the hypothesis of a final option makes clear why Christ chose to save humankind by his death rather than in any other manner. "Christ's human reality . . . reaches the perfection of its instrumentality only in death, for—as the hypothesis of a final decision suggests—nothing that is human comes to the fully complete positing of its reality until it does so in death."[28]

In two of his later works, Boros returns to the themes of *The Mystery of Death.*[29] He describes both volumes as meditations centering on the joyful dimension of life and the promise for the future. Humanity's interior or personal growth is brought to fulfillment in the act of death. "In death comes the possibility of man's fully personal action. Consequently death is the point of full consciousness, freedom, and decision regarding one's eternal lot."[30] Thus, every human being has the potential to decide for or against Christ in the full possession of his or her powers. At the moment of death, Christ stands before the person, "luminously perceived, summoning him to himself." The individual makes his or her ultimate decision in that fully personal encounter with Christ. However, we simply cannot move through life thoughtlessly, postponing our destiny until the moment of final decision.

Boros insists that our death is also our purgatory wherein we encounter Christ and must sustain "the fire of his gazing love, which is our ultimate purification." This process of purification—which differs in intensity for each—involves the most grievous suffering, reaching down to the very marrow of our being.[31] According to Boros, since the soul cannot exist without a body, the resurrection must take place at the moment of death. At that moment the soul enters into what he calls a "pancosmic relationship" with the universe and becomes present everywhere in the cosmos. The transformation that is realized on the last day with Christ's second coming brings about the completion of the resurrection that begins at death. For Boros, the risen human being needs the transformed universe as its proper dwelling place. "Thus the human soul is never without a body; immortality and resurrection are one and the same."[32]

He continues to emphasize that the possibility of an individual's first fully personal decision occurs in death, for this is when we attain our full awareness. At that moment we become capable of a total, undistracted encounter with God in Christ, and of making a definitive decision about him.[33] In death we reach our full adulthood and become capable of making an ultimate decision.[34] At this point we become wholly ourselves and complete persons. Boros affirms, however, that we must strive in life to achieve that degree of resoluteness that will allow us to make the right decisions in death. While Jesus often describes the happiness of eternal life as an intimate union with God, Boros holds out the possibility of hell for those who choose to be satisfied in themselves forever.

Joseph Ratzinger (1927–)

A professor of theology for eight years at the University of Regensburg, Joseph Ratzinger became archbishop of Munich in 1977. In 1981 he was appointed Prefect of the Doctrine of the Faith Office in Rome. His treatise on eschatology was published in German in 1977 and appeared in English in 1988.[35] Ratzinger attests that the subject of eschatology has lately become a critical topic for biblicists and theologians. He objects to the fact that the discipline is concentrated currently on the theology of hope and the theology of liberation, thus neglecting the classical themes of the "last things." During the Middle Ages, attention was focused on personal salvation rather than on the sweep of salvation history as a whole. Ratzinger asserts that the role of the theologian today is to blend the theme of personal salvation with the treatment of the ultimate destiny of the cosmos. The one direction must be complemented by the other. The more traditional eschatology focusing on personal salvation must now be seen in the context of the future of all creation.

There is no doubt about the fact that an indispensable component of Jesus' preaching was the anticipation of an imminent end. He proclaimed himself as the one who delivers ultimate salvation. "For, in fact, the kingdom of God is among you" (Luke 17:21). He identifies himself as the eschatological sign of God (Luke 11:20). The New Testament does contain references to the imminent end. In Matthew, for example, the end of time is announced along with the destruction of Jerusalem (chap. 24), creating the impression of imminence. Also, Jesus is quoted as saying that there are some among his current disciples "who will not taste death before they see the Son of Man coming in his kingdom" (Matt 16:28). The expectation of the end is viewed as less imminent in Luke and Mark. As a matter of fact, in 2 Peter 3:4 the urgency is softened considerably. Although the kingdom is a central theme of Jesus' preaching, in the post-Easter proclamation, the leitmotiv is Christology.

Ratzinger summarizes the approaches of such twentieth-century scholars as Karl Barth, Rudolf Bultmann, and Oscar Cullmann, and he criticizes Jürgen Moltmann for transforming eschatology into political theology. The kingdom of God for Ratzinger is a charter not for political activity but for moral activity.[36] The kingdom that Christ promises is not aimed at the transformation of our economic or political circumstances. Rather, its purpose is the development of sons and daughters of God. "The message of Jesus cannot make its peace with any eschatology principally emphasizing changed living conditions."[37]

Ratzinger then directs his attention to the theology of death, which he claims has been largely ignored by our bourgeois society. In the Old Testament death is not viewed as annihilation, although Sheol is portrayed as a kind of unlife. Yahweh is absent and the souls in Sheol are described as shades. Daniel 12:1–2 represents the clearest articulation of Old Testament faith in the resurrection, along with 2 Maccabees, chapters 6 and 7. In the New Testament death is everywhere seen as the entrance into a new life wherein the just will live with God and the unrepentant will be deprived forever of the divine presence.

He then investigates the relationship between the immortality of the human soul and the resurrection of the dead. In response to much that he reads in twentieth-century theology, Ratzinger asks how the long tradition of the souls' immortality can be so quickly overthrown.[38] He concedes that the idea that the resurrection takes place at the moment of death has become quite popular. How this can be imagined without any connection with matter is puzzling to him. How can there be a bodily resurrection without corporeality? For Ratzinger the message of Jesus' resurrection on the third day places a definite time period between the death of Christ and his resurrection. Thus, he rejects the notion of resurrection immediately after death. Ratzinger's conception of the intermediate state is grounded in the belief that the soul is immortal and survives beyond the death of the body. He also rejects the notion of a sleep of death, that is, an unconscious state between death and the parousia. He affirms that those who have died in Christ are somehow alive in him. All the ancient creeds proclaim the resurrection of the body (or the flesh), and the Provincial Council of Toledo XI in 675 notes that we shall rise with our self-same flesh.[39] Although it is difficult to envision, the Fourth Lateran Council issued the same declaration in 1215.[40] Ratzinger affirms that Benedict XII's constitution, *Benedictus Deus* in 1336, insists that the souls of the departed who have been purified are taken up into heaven even before they are reunited with their bodies.[41]

According to Ratzinger, it was at this time that purgatory became part of the Catholic tradition. Martin Luther rejected the immortality of the soul and held to the notion of the corporeal resurrection after death.[42] The concept of the soul's immortality was fully set out by Aquinas (d. 1274), and it was the Council of Vienne (1312) that identified the soul as the substantial form of the body. For Ratzinger resurrection at the moment of death is not well founded in the Scriptures.[43] In spite of the wasting away of the body in death, it is the whole person, that is, the human soul, who moves on toward eternity. However, we are not able to extrapolate from our present life to the nature and character of the life to come. "The content of eternal life . . . lies completely outside the scope of our experience."[44]

Ratzinger asks how some scholars can place the resurrection at the moment of death despite the fact that a human being does not rise bodily at that point. It seems essential that the resurrection must have something to do with matter. In 1 Corinthians 15:35–54 Paul discusses how the dead are raised and what sort of bodies they will possess. He does not maintain that the risen body is identical with one's earthly body, as though the risen life were but a continuation of our present existence. He emphasizes frequently the christological quality of the risen life but offers no real explanation of the nature of that life. Although Ratzinger concedes that resurrection in the subapostolic period often had reference to the resurrection of the body, he claims that since Aquinas, the faith consensus prefers that the resurrection of the body will occur at the parousia. This would mean that the Thomistic teaching would hardly be able to preserve the identity between our earthly and our risen bodies.

Our participation in the heavenly kingdom will not occur until the guilt we have left behind is removed through our purgatorial suffering.

True enough, the decisive outcome of each person's life is settled in death, at the close of his earthly activity. Thus everyone is judged and reaches his definitive destiny after death.
But his final place in the whole can be determined only when
the total organism is complete, when the *passio* and *actio* of
history have come to their end. And so the gathering together
of the whole will be an act that leaves no person unaffected.
Only at that juncture can the definitive general judgment
take place, judging each man in terms of the whole and giving him that just place which he can receive only in conjunc-
tion with all the rest.[45]

Ratzinger remains open to the position of Karl Rahner that at death,
the soul becomes "pancosmic," and thus its essential ordination to the
material world is preserved. We are discouraged by Ratzinger, however,
from speculating aimlessly regarding the final destiny of the universe,
for "the new world cannot be imagined nor can the risen body."[46]

The signs in the Gospel of Mark that foretell the end—false mes-
siahs, wars, earthquakes, and famine—will come when they will come,
and we do not know when. Therefore, every age must be watchful.
"Beware, keep alert; for you do not know when the time will come"
(Mark 13:33). The one precondition that must precede the end is the
proclamation of the gospel to all the nations (v. 10). In chapters 9
through 11 of Romans, Paul also insists that the conversion of the Jews
to Christ must occur before the final days. Ratzinger insists that the last
judgment cannot be visualized by us in spite of the several New
Testament portrayals of the scene. He allows for the everlasting banishment of those who have distanced themselves from Christ, for this
is the price of those who have enclosed themselves away from God.
The Deity is portrayed as inflicting perdition on no one, for each person is responsible for his or her own judgment. The thesis of the final
option (Ladislaus Boros) troubles Ratzinger. For him, humans do not
have to enjoy angelic freedom to choose heaven or hell in a definitive
manner. Human freedom is more than adequate for us to determine
our eternal destiny.

In taking a stand against Origen's universal reconciliation, Ratzinger
reminds us that this position is no more than a hypothesis that he
himself rejects. Although Gregory of Nyssa, Didymus of Alexandria,
Theodore of Mopsuestia, and others espoused the view of Origen,
Ratzinger reminds us that mainstream tradition did not.[47] Christ does

not treat humans as immature beings who lack responsibility for deciding their eternal future. Thus, for Ratzinger the doctrine of ever-lasting punishment endures. The same can be said of the existence of purgatory. Although the Greeks rejected the idea of temporal punishment in the life after death, they have always honored the practice of praying for the dead. Also, the Reformers were not able to accept the existence of temporary atonement in the life to come.[48]

Heaven, for Ratzinger, is participation in the risen Lord's place at the right hand of the Father. It is an individual experience for each, for everyone sees and experiences God in his or her own proper way. The vision of God involves an immediacy between God and the person, and thus the individual enters upon his or her boundless fulfillment.[49] However, the salvation of the individual is only complete when the salvation of the cosmos and all of the elect has been achieved.

An appendix was added to the work in 1979 after the publication of *A Letter on Certain Questions in Eschatology* by the Doctrine of the Faith Office in May 1979. In short, the Roman document reaffirms the traditional Catholic view that human beings who die in God's favor live with the Lord even before the corporeal resurrection that does not occur until the last days. Ratzinger, who was then archbishop of Munich, expressed full and total acceptance of the Roman declaration. He added that Vatican II (1962–65) left many scholars with the impression that Christian doctrine in all its aspects was to be sketched out anew.[50] Ratzinger criticized the Dutch Catechism that appeared within a year after the close of the council because it made light of the doctrine of the immortality of the soul, "substituting in its place a remarkably obscure anthropology of resurrection by stages."[51] The archbishop insisted that the doctrine of the immortality of the soul, defined by Lateran V in 1513, remains absolutely obligatory, and any attempt to dilute it amounts to a rupture in the continuity of tradition.[52]

Ratzinger's second appendix was added as an afterword to the English edition in 1987. At that time he was Cardinal Prefect of the Doctrine of the Faith Office in Rome. This brief statement reemphasizes the need to affirm the immortality of the human soul, since the biblical data can only find appropriate expression in this manner. Once again he urges that eschatology should not be changed into a political theology or into a generalized theology of hope.[53] Finally, he apologizes to his English readers, noting that because of his busy schedule, he was unable to study the English language literature "with that serenity and patience necessary to re-do the work for English readers."[54]

Observations

Karl Rahner affirms that from the first Christian centuries the church has made assertions regarding the future that have left much that is hidden and obscure. With death we become integrated with the universe, and our spiritual reality becomes part of the world. The resurrection of the body constitutes the completion of our entrance into the new life when matter and spirit are reunited. For Boros it is only in death that we humans can make a fully personal decision that determines our ultimate destiny. In Ratzinger's judgment, we cannot envision the possibility of the bodily resurrection occurring immediately after death. He builds a strong case for purgatory to prepare us for our life with God, and he unequivocally rejects Origen's notion of universal restoration.

NOTES

1. Karl Rahner, *Faith in a Wintery Season* (ed. P. Imhof and H. Biallowons; trans. R. Teske; New York: Crossroad, 1991), 39.
2. Karl Rahner, *On the Theology of Death* (trans. Charles H. Henkey; New York: Herder & Herder, 1961), 29.
3. Ibid., 53.
4. Ibid., 74.
5. Ibid., 77.
6. Karl Rahner, "The Resurrection of the Body," trans. Karl H. Kruger, in *Theological Investigations* (vol. 2; Baltimore: Helicon Press, 1963), 205.
7. Ibid., 211.
8. Ibid., 215.
9. Ibid., 215–16.
10. Karl Rahner, "The Hermeneutics of Eschatological Assertions," trans. Kevin Smyth, in *Theological Investigations* (vol. 4; Baltimore: Helicon Press, 1966), 324.
11. Ibid., 330.
12. Ibid., 340.
13. Karl Rahner, *Foundations of Christian Faith* (trans. William V. Dych; New York: Crossroad, 1986), 431.
14. Ibid., 434.
15. Ibid., 436.
16. Karl Rahner, "Eschatology," *Encyclopedia of Theology: The Concise Sacramentum Mundi* (ed. Karl Rahner; New York: Crossroad, 1975), 434–35.

17. Leo J. Donovan, "Living with Mystery: Karl Rahner's Reflections at 75," *America* 140, no. 9 (10 March 1979): 179.

18. Ladislaus Boros, *The Moment of Truth: Mysterium Mortis* (trans. Gregory Bainbridge; London: Burns & Oates, 1965).

19. Ibid., ix.

20. Ibid., 23.

21. Ibid., 28–29.

22. Ibid., 62.

23. Ibid., 84.

24. Ibid., 97.

25. Ibid., 105.

26. Ibid., 115.

27. Ibid., 155.

28. Ibid., 168.

29. Ladislaus Boros, *Living in Hope* (trans. W. J. O'Hara; New York: Herder & Herder, 1968); *We Are Future* (trans. W. J. O'Hara; New York: Herder & Herder, 1970).

30. Boros, *Living in Hope*, 22.

31. Ibid., 29.

32. Ibid., 34.

33. Boros, *We Are Future*, 157.

34. Ibid., 164.

35. Joseph Ratzinger, *Eschatology—Death and Eternal Life* (trans. Michael Waldstein; ed. Aidan Nichols; Washington, D.C.: Catholic University of America Press, 1988).

36. Ibid., 58.

37. Ibid., 69.

38. Ibid., 105.

39. H. Denzinger and A. Schönmetzer, *Enchiridion Symbolorum* (32d ed.; Freiburg: Herder, 1963), no. 540.

40. Ibid., no. 801.

41. Ibid., no. 1000.

42. Ratzinger, *Eschatology*, 139.

43. Ibid., 160.

44. Ibid., 161.

45. Ibid., 190.

46. Ibid., 192.

47. Ibid., 216.

48. Ibid., 219.

49. Ibid., 235.

50. Ibid., 248.

51. Ibid., 249.
52. Denzinger and Schönmetzer, *Enchiridion Symbolorum,* no. 1440.
53. Ibid., 273.
54. Ibid., 273–74.

4

KÜNG, HELLWIG, AND VON BALTHASAR: OTHER RECENT COMPLEMENTARY VISIONS OF ESCHATOLOGY

Hans Küng (1928-)

The theological training of Hans Küng began in the fall of 1951 at the Gregorian University in Rome. In 1957 he completed his doctoral studies at the Institut Catholique in Paris. That year he began his teaching career at the University of Tübingen where he has worked ever since. In 1985 the English edition of his study *Eternal Life?* was published, a work that had appeared in German three years earlier. Küng states that "theology cannot avoid the demand for verification of belief in eternity."[1]

The Greek philosopher Plato worked tirelessly to discover new arguments for the soul's immortality. He based his approach on the fact that the soul is simple, spiritual, and in a sense divine. Augustine followed Plato as did Aquinas, Descartes, and Leibniz. It was Immanuel Kant who taught that although the immortality of the soul, like the existence of God, cannot be demonstrated, it is what he called a postulate of the practical reason, for it is an indispensable precondition for the ethical behavior of human beings. Küng teaches that if belief in the soul's immortality is not demonstrable, we can show that it is well founded since it is based on human experience. With our experience as the horizon and the biblical message as the ground, we have reasonable justification for belief in eternal life.[2]

Küng conceded that it is impossible to refute someone such as Freud who insists that death is the end of everything. However, based on our experience, we have adequate justification for affirming the reality of life after death, for without this belief, life seems to many to be pointless. Our commitment then to eternal life is a matter of reasonable trust, which Küng describes as faith in a life beyond. The Old

Testament Book of Qoheleth (Ecclesiastes), composed in 190–180 B.C., is very different from Proverbs and Sirach (early second century B.C.), both of which hold out hope for the future. Ecclesiastes is shot through with skepticism. We are simply born to die, with little hope for a positive hereafter. The whole human being lives on, however, as a shade or ghost in Sheol. Toward the end of the Old Testament period, the Book of Daniel (12:2) and 2 Maccabees (chaps. 7 and 8) teach the resurrection of the dead, which was never clearly affirmed in the Old Testament before the second century B.C. After the Babylonian exile, the Jews became dissatisfied with the traditional belief that all life ends with the grave, save for the shadowy stay in Sheol. The work of Proverbs and Sirach thus paved the way for the Book of Daniel and 2 Maccabees.

Küng spends a considerable amount of time analyzing the resurrection of Jesus. Although the essential elements are present in all New Testament accounts, the variations in the narratives can be explained by the diversity of authors and the time and place of the writings. Paul's narrative in 1 Corinthians 15 has the sound of an official rendering of the event, which is not portrayed as a historical happening but which does have the flavor of a real occurrence to which one can commit with reasonable trust.[3] The resurrection, then, is a happening of faith, and Paul attests that because Christ has been raised up, there will be a universal resurrection (1 Cor 15:21–22). However, it is difficult for us to imagine the resurrection of the body, which can be identified as a transformation of the whole person by the Spirit. Küng describes death as a passing into God, a retreat into the innermost primal ground, out of the darkness and into God's eternal light.[4] Resurrection stands as the critical test of our faith.

Küng prefers to describe the ascension of Christ as the taking up of Jesus into God's life. In 1 Peter we read that after the resurrection Christ went to issue a proclamation to the spirits in prison (3:18–20).

A number of vague New Testament texts indicate that Christ, presumably after his death, descended beneath the earth (Rom. 10:7; Eph. 4:9), that he took up from below dead saints (Matt. 27:52; Eph. 4:8), and that he triumphed over the evil angelic powers (Phil. 2:10; Col. 2:15). . . . From the fourth century to the sixth an article was making its way into the Apostles' Creed: "He descended into hell." The clause is a curiosity in the sense that the church has never decided the exact purpose of that journey. . . . [I]t is a way of expressing figuratively that Christ's death affected those who had gone before.[5]

Küng mentions that the *Symbol Quicumque* (the Athanasian Creed) affirms that the fires of hell are indeed eternal. This important document, apparently composed in the fifth or sixth century in southern Gaul, was extremely influential in the development of popular faith in the West.[6] The Fourth Lateran Council (1215) declared that the punishment of those in hell is eternal.[7] Even more explicit and fearsome was the pronouncement of the Council of Florence (1442), which spoke of the throngs of souls in hell—including nonbelievers, heretics, schismatics, and Jews.[8]

When Jesus spoke of hell on occasion, his words were simply couched in the imagery of his time. No special truths or insights were revealed by him regarding the nature of the hereafter. He mentioned hell only marginally and in the customary language of the day. Küng prefers to refer to the notion of purgatory as a process of purification, and he views it as an encounter with God who judges and purifies. Perhaps the New Testament references to hellfire could be nothing more than metaphors to keep persons on track lest they miss the ultimate meaning of life.[9] The idea of universal restoration *(apokatástasis pantōn)* has been occasionally proposed by theologians since the time of Origen (ca. 185–253). It is possible that it is only what Küng calls a superficial universalism—in which all are saved from the outset—that does not do justice to the seriousness of life. For him heaven is not to be described as something above or beyond. Rather, it is a mode of existing in being within the incomprehensible sphere of God. Heaven should not be envisioned as located on earth, nor does Küng teach that we are called on to create heaven on earth.[10]

The biblical picture of the general judgment on the last day is beyond our imagination, given the prospect of billions of persons who would be present. However, the image of the last judgment can still speak to us concerning the cosmic dimension of human destiny. The ultimate question that Küng raises is whether or not all will be saved. Although the New Testament narratives occasionally portray a division of humanity into the saved and the condemned, Paul suggests a final mercy for all.[11] Küng points to Isaiah 65:17–25, the portrait of the new heaven and the new earth, as one of the richest and most impressive pictures of the end time, as well as of the timeless and imperishable life with God.

And what if there is nothing beyond? Küng insists that we are confident that all of human life will not end in a void, and our hope for absolute meaning will be realized.[12] "God then will not merely be in everything, as he is now, but truly all in all . . . transforming everything into himself because he gives to all a share in his eternal life in unrestricted, endless fullness."[13]

In 1992 Hans Küng published a popular piece on the Apostles' Creed that appeared in English one year later.[14] Returning to the subject of the last things, he reasserts that heaven can best be described as the invisible, incomprehensible sphere of God. Although the images depicting the final judgment of the world in the New Testament can hardly be taken literally, the biblical notion of judgment cannot be abandoned. Küng feels that world history requires a final, definitive accounting. Regarding the devil and his minions, there is no doubt that there is an evil influence in the world that transcends individuals. The personification of evil, however, in terms of Satan and his cohorts springs out of the Persian dualism that the Hebrews in all probability assimilated into their religious ethos during their stay in Babylon in the sixth century B.C. This has remained a part of our Judeo-Christian tradition.

Regarding the eternal duration of hell affirmed by the medieval church documents summarized above, Küng reminds his readers that such notable theologians as Origen, Gregory of Nyssa, and Jerome taught that the punishments of hell are imposed on the evil ones only for a time.[15] Since the Enlightenment and the development of the modern systems of criminal justice, the notion of endless or eternal punishment has become for all intents and purposes intolerable. Even the *sensus fidelium* (the judgment of the faithful) is moving away from it.

> In the eternal punishment (Matt. 25:46) of the Last Judgment the emphasis lies on the fact that this punishment is definitive, final, decisive for ever, not that the torment must last eternally. . . . [I]t is a contradiction to accept God's love and mercy and at the same time the existence of a place of eternal torment. No, the punishment of hell, like everything else, remains subordinate to God, his will and his grace.[16]

Küng teaches that purgatory as an intermediate phase of cleansing after death really has no basis in the Scriptures. He is convinced that the unexpiated guilt can very well be remitted in the process of death itself. What purifies the individual is the actual encounter with God in the passage of death. We must continue to pray for the dying, commending them lovingly to the Lord. But "this doesn't mean that some superstitious lifelong prayer . . . is required for particular 'poor souls' in purgatory."[17]

Will everyone be saved at the end? On the one hand Küng cannot completely agree with the thesis of Origen that all will surely be saved, nor can he agree with Calvin that some are irrevocably destined for damnation. Paul's promise that "one man's act of righteousness leads to justification and life for all" (Rom 5:18) gives us some hope that all will somehow be saved in the end. However, Küng concedes that this issue must remain open. He warns, though, that those who take their personal responsibility too lightly must be aware that their salvation is not a priori guaranteed.[18]

Monika K. Hellwig (1929–)

A professor at Georgetown University for three decades, Monika Hellwig had a special interest in eschatology. In 1978 she published a popular piece, *What Are They Saying about Death and Christian Hope?*[19] She notes the shift in emphasis from individual eschatology to what she calls general eschatology in recent authors, for example, Moltmann and Pannenberg. Further, she asserts that new questions surrounding the meaning of Christian hope are being asked in different ways, and that a new consensus regarding these issues is some years away. One of the most frequently asked questions today centers around what happens to us after death and how much we can control the events we will encounter after death. She affirms that recently a pessimism has undermined "even the more modest hopes and expectations of former times."[20] Some have wondered whether life makes any sense at all. One of the core questions is, Why must we die? We are dealing here with the unknown, because death has never been experienced by any of us, and hence the challenge to come to grips with it is enormous.

Among Christians of the early centuries, the resurrection of the dead gradually gave way to the notion of the immortality of the soul, which at death is released from the imprisonment of the body. Hell was viewed as a place of intolerable torment, and heaven the destination of the just who enjoy the beatific vision. In modern times these portrayals take on a strange and rather uncomfortable cast since there is no way of verifying them. Also, if the soul is considered the life principle of the human person, how can we imagine it functioning if it is not supported by the brain and the nervous system? Thus, the continuing existence of the separated soul is not especially easy to imagine.

If the person is the living body and we can observe that the human body decays and breaks up to become the substance for other organic things that have their own life and their own quality of livingness, then one cannot easily predicate the survival of the person beyond death.[21]

Hellwig suggests that there could well be in death a transition of consciousness "from being rooted in the individual body to being rooted in the community."[22] This, however, is simply speculation that may or may not be valid.

Since the official church teachings left most of the biblical imagery untouched, we now have to search behind the poetic language to discern the true meaning of the statements regarding the last things. We must understand death as a moment when our lives receive their ultimate destination, which occurs at the moment referred to as the particular judgment. Hellwig attests that the idea of reincarnation seems to be ruled out by the belief that our final destiny is once and for all determined at death. "Purgatory is presented as the completion or fulfillment of options already made and not fully implemented."[23] Since many of the just do not reach the state of perfect charity in life, the doctrine of purgatory responds to that situation by providing for the attainment of perfect love. Hellwig affirms that the purgatorial purification within the process of death seems preferable to the idea of purgatory as a time span of some sort. She also holds to the irrevocability of damnation inasmuch as we are totally responsible for the destiny and final outcome of our lives. The notion of eternity "seems to be intended to underscore this irrevocability and totality."[24] Hellwig reminds us, however, that it has never been officially taught that any human persons were or would be in hell.

The resurrection of Jesus is by no means a simple return to his previous earthly life. Rather, it is a transformation into a new mode of existence and presence. The New Testament testimonies reveal the new life that had come forth among Christ's followers as a totally revitalized reality within themselves. For example, the earliest Christians spoke of having risen with the Lord. They were animated with a new boldness and a new energy for taking up their mission of evangelization. "What this cumulative experience gives us are reasonable grounds of credibility and solid grounds of hope for a passage through death to a heightened and intensified life."[25] There also remain serious concerns regarding our belief in a bodily resurrection, which has always been attested by Christians. The person is not to be seen as an embodied soul but as a living body that is the very expression of our personal existence. Hellwig does not speculate on the condition of human souls during the period when they are no longer in the body, for speculation leads to nothing more than poetic projections. "If we do not know what to expect beyond death in any factual way, death places the absolute exigence to make sense of the life that we do know within the dimensions and terms of that life as we know it."[26]

The present tendency to focus on cosmic eschatology rather than individual eschatology does redirect our search for individual salvation in terms of the primacy of charity, and our need to contribute to the growth and enrichment of the human community. Hellwig emphasizes that there is a continuity between personal salvation and our contribution to the redemption of the whole human family.

> The New Testament and traditional church teachings emphasize the certainty of hope beyond death and despair on the one hand, but insist on leaving the content of the promises in figurative imagery on the other hand. The hope is important, but the control of the hope cannot be systematically deciphered—this is what the church teaching appears in the last analysis to say.[27]

Hellwig wrote the section on eschatology for the two-volume treatise *Systematic Theology,* edited by Francis Schüssler Fiorenza and John P. Galvin and which appeared in 1991.[28] She states that general eschatology became less important after Constantine and that the original imagery portraying individual eschatology was taken quite literally until modern times. The ancient symbols were simply repeated from century to century, and as a result the discipline remained rather underdeveloped. Within the last several generations, this presentation became less and less acceptable to sensitive believers because it seemed out of step with the currents of the age. General eschatology, on the other hand, grew in importance, for it aims at the restructuring of the present order and emphasizes our social responsibility. The goal of eschatology came to be focused on the salvation of the world.

Our individualistic culture, however, clamors for answers to the old questions surrounding the content of our personal Christian hopes. Heaven continues to be viewed as the ultimate happiness intended for all, while the everlasting character of the sufferings of hell remains, according to Hellwig, an integral part of the New Testament message. Purgatory belongs to the content of our faith because most individuals after death are not ready to enter into the divine presence without a preparation of some sort. Hellwig closes, however, with a reminder that the overriding message upon which we must fix our eyes and hearts is God's universal salvific will.

Hans Urs von Balthasar (1905–88)

After obtaining his doctorate in German studies and philosophy at the University of Berlin, Hans Urs von Balthasar entered the Jesuits in 1929. He received his theological training at Pullach and Lyons. While remaining in the Catholic ministry, he left the Jesuits in 1950 to establish a secular institute with Adrienne von Speyer.[29] In the field of eschatology, Balthasar continually stresses God's saving will that is extended to all of humanity. Although he did not espouse Origen's position of universal restoration, he did emphasize again and again that we must hold out hope that God will save all. In 1986 Balthasar published the short study *Dare We Hope "That All Men Be Saved"?* and added a brief piece on hell in 1987. The two monographs were originally published in German and made available in English in 1988.[30]

Balthasar affirms that there are two series of New Testament statements regarding the question of ultimate human destiny. The first group, the pre-Easter sayings, envision the real possibility of salvation or condemnation for humankind. Matthew 25 dramatically portrays this twofold outcome. Other passages in the Synoptics assume the same twofold destiny for humans (e.g., Mark 16:16). However, Balthasar points out that there is a second series of post-Easter sayings that proclaims that the saving grace of God will be available and operative in all. Romans 11:32 announces that God will be merciful to all since he earnestly desires that all will be saved. In the Gospel of John, Jesus promises that when he is lifted up from the earth, he will draw all to himself (12:32). Indeed, everyone who believes in him has eternal life and does not come under judgment (5:24). Although Balthasar affirms that the pre-Easter and post-Easter assertions cannot be merged into "a readily comprehensible system," he continues to emphasize that it is God's will that all be saved.[31]

It was Origen (ca. 185–253) who was the first among the Fathers to speak of salvation for all. Balthasar notes that Cyprian (ca. 200–258) seems to suggest that no Christians, even though they had sinned grievously, would be dispatched to hell. The same view was held by Hilary of Poiters (ca. 315–67) and can be found in the early writings of Jerome (348–420). Others who proposed the doctrine of universal salvation were Clement of Alexandria (ca. 150–215), Gregory of Nyssa (ca. 335–94), and more discreetly by Gregory of Nazianzus (330–89) and Maximus the Confessor (580–662).[32] It was Augustine of Hippo (354–430) who insisted on the twofold outcome as the only correct interpretation, and all in the West followed his lead from Pope Gregory the Great (590–604) to Thomas Aquinas (1225–74). The Athanasian Creed (latter fifth century), which embodied the Augustinian point of view, firmly professed the twofold destiny of either heaven or hell that is the lot of all. This pattern was repeated at Lateran IV (1215), Lyons I and II (1245, 1274), and Florence (1439). These conciliar statements are described by Balthasar as simply the reformulations of Matthew 25.[33] Origen seems to have been the first to question the eternity of hell, and he holds out the hypothetical possibility of a return to grace even on the part of the devil and his cohorts. His hypothesis is based largely on 1 Corinthians 3:11–15, which he paraphrases in the following manner:

"[A]ll men on the last day, will have to go through fire, and that, depending on whether they have or have not built on Christ's foundation, their work will survive or burn, while they themselves will be saved, but only as through fire."[34] The Reformers and the Jansenists also followed Augustine, who devoted all of book 21 of his *City of God* to the various punishments of hell. Balthasar attests that Augustine's clear and repeated insistence on the twofold outcome—either heaven or hell—set the tone for theology up to recent times. "The door was firmly closed and carefully fitted with many bolts; and, for the theology of posterity, it has long remained locked."[35]

Karl Barth insisted that Jesus was condemned for the sake of sinners so that all sinners can be redeemed. According to Balthasar, the many disclaimers that Barth does not affirm a position of *apokatástasis pantōn* are really only rhetorical.[36] Since the nineteenth century many theologians have struggled with the problem of an everlasting hell, while others have been so angered by the idea of eternal punishment that they no longer wish to serve so harsh a judge.[37] In the Middle Ages individuals such as Bernard of Clairvaux (1090–1153) and Anselm of Canterbury (1033–1109) made every effort to give priority to the mercy of God, but the momentum of the Augustinian tradition stressing the twofold outcome was too strong to overcome. Anselm taught that sparing evildoers is every bit as just as punishing them, but the awful prospect of hell and eternal damnation had become embedded in the very marrow of the Christian tradition.

Balthasar adamantly refused to teach that a certain number of individuals are actually languishing in the fires of hell. Although he wants us to view the loss of heaven as a possibility, he notes how ironic it is that church tradition has never asserted that any individual has actually been consigned to hell. Balthasar prefers to stand with those who emphasize the mercy of God over all. He declares, "I think it permissible to hope (on the basis of the first series of statements from Scripture) that the light of divine love will ultimately be able to penetrate every human darkness and refusal."[38] All the positive New Testament declarations (e.g., John 12:32; Rom 5:18; Col 1:20; 1 Tim 2:4) give us a claim to hope for the salvation of all humankind. Thus, Balthasar insists, "I see no need to take the step from the threats [implied in the statements reflecting the outcome of heaven or hell] to the positing of a hell occupied by our brothers and sisters."[39]

We are reminded by Balthasar that the word *apokatástasis* appears only once in the New Testament, in Peter's sermon delivered in the Jerusalem temple (Acts 3:21). The verse alludes to the return of Jesus who is to "remain in heaven until the time of universal restoration that God announced long ago through his holy prophets." The term in this context has no clear reference to the ultimate salvation of all, but Origen offered this verse as the ground for his tentative theory regarding the subject. Gregory of Nyssa concurred with Origen, and Maximus the Confessor offered a modified version of Origen's hypothesis. Gregory reasoned that the pains of hell could not be coeternal with God because of the essential superiority of good over evil,[40] Maximus's position was qualified with utmost care because of the vigorous condemnation of Origen's view at Constantinople II (553).

In the fifth volume of his *Theo-Drama*, Balthasar deals with the events of the last days as outlined in the New Testament. This final volume of what could be considered his masterpiece was published in German in 1983 and appeared in English in 1998.[41] He outlines in some detail the events of the end time as described in the New Testament. In those days there will be a dramatic increase of antagonism between the kingdom of Christ and the kingdom of Satan, who in the end will present himself as the Antichrist. When Christ comes again he will destroy the "lawless one" (2 Thess 2:3–12). Then will follow the general resurrection, and after that the judgment. No one knows when these events will occur except the Father. However, we are warned in Mark 13:10 that before the end, the gospel must be preached to all the nations.

Balthasar returns to the subject of the salvation of all, and concedes that this position calls for the reevaluation of a good number of biblical passages that speak of the twofold outcome, whereby all are destined either to heaven or to hell. Schleiermacher affirmed that since many New Testament passages speak of universal salvation, we must give this view an equal right to exist. Karl Barth remained open to the possibility of universal restoration just as long as the thesis of the twofold outcome is not positively excluded.[42] According to von Balthasar, all of Jesus' statements referring to the possibility of eternal condemnation are what he calls pre-Easter words. The post-Easter declarations of John and Paul primarily stress the universality of redemption, although Paul does distinguish those who are saved from those who are condemned (1 Cor 1:18).[43] In spite of Balthasar's recurring emphasis on the ultimate salvation of all, he does remind us that even in the post-Easter statements there is an occasional suggestion of the twofold outcome.

Balthasar offers the opinion that both the Old and the New Testaments speak of only one judgment.[44] This will occur on the last day when all the deeds of humankind will be examined in great detail. In Jesus' day there was the expectation of a general resurrection of the dead at the end of the world, and the judgment would take place at that time. There was also the opinion in the primitive church that certain privileged souls, such as the martyrs, would be taken up into the presence of God immediately after death.[45] Balthasar finds the twofold judgment—particular and general—to be unacceptable. For him the one judgment takes place alongside the course of world history, while the fire of testing, which he calls purgatory, is doing its work. "Purgatory ends [for the individual] at the precise point where man, looking at the Cross, begins to realize the extent of the world's sin, which somewhere or other contains his own sin."[46] In this manner, all of humankind will be brought into definitive discipleship with Christ.

Observations

Hans Küng declares that a superficial understanding of universal salvation, whereby all are saved from the very outset, does not do justice to the seriousness of life. He feels that the general judgment involving billions of people is beyond our imagination yet cannot be abandoned. To him the eternity of hell is intolerable, for it is a contradiction in light of God's mercy. Küng asks whether all will be saved, as Paul on occasion intimates, and his response is that the issue must be left open.

For Monika Hellwig the existence of the separated soul, as well as the risen body, is difficult to imagine. She insists on the eternity of hell but asks if anyone is there. Purgatory is surely a part of our faith heritage, for most are not ready at death to enter the divine presence. Although there has been a shift in recent years from individual to cosmic eschatology, she believes that we are far from reaching a consensus regarding the direction of this discipline.

Balthasar attests that there are two series of New Testament sayings that must be dealt with. Those that emphasize the dual outcome of life—heaven or hell—are mostly pre-Easter sayings, while those emphasizing the salvation of all are post-Easter statements found primarily in John and Paul. It was Augustine who set the course for the prevalence of the twofold outcome scenario in the West. However, Balthasar insists that it is indeed permissible to hope for the salvation of all.

NOTES

1. Hans Küng, *Eternal Life?* (trans. Edward Quinn; New York: Doubleday, 1985), 73.
2. Ibid., 76.
3. Ibid., 105.
4. Ibid., 113.
5. Raymond Brown, *An Introduction to the New Testament* (New York: Doubleday, 1997), 714–15.
6. H. Denzinger and A. Schönmetzer, *Enchiridion Symbolorum* (32d ed.; Freiburg: Herder, 1963), no. 76.
7. Ibid., no. 801.
8. Ibid., no. 1351.
9. Küng, *Eternal Life?* 140.
10. Ibid., 199.
11. Ibid., 212.
12. Ibid., 231.
13. Ibid., 233.
14. Hans Küng, *Credo: The Apostles' Creed Explained for Today* (trans. John Bowden; New York: Doubleday, 1993).
15. Ibid., 174.
16. Ibid., 175–76.
17. Ibid., 177.
18. Ibid., 179.

19. Monika K. Hellwig, *What Are They Saying about Death and Christian Hope?* (New York: Paulist Press, 1978).

20. Ibid., 10.

21. Ibid., 20.

22. Ibid., 21.

23. Ibid., 25.

24. Ibid., 31.

25. Ibid., 40.

26. Ibid., 45.

27. Ibid., 64.

28. Monika K. Hellwig, "Eschatology," in *Systematic Theology: Roman Catholic Perspectives* (vol. 2; ed. Francis Schüssler Fiorenza and John P. Galvin; Minneapolis: Fortress, 1991), 349–72.

29. A secular institute is a comparatively recent canonical community wherein vows are taken but the members live ordinary lives in the world.

30. Hans Urs von Balthasar, *Dare We Hope "That All Men Be Saved"?* (trans. David Kipp and Lothar Krauth; San Francisco: Ignatius Press, 1988).

31. Ibid., 44–45.

32. Ibid., 63.

33. Ibid., 48.

34. Ibid., 60.

35. Ibid., 69.

36. Ibid., 94.

37. Ibid., 120.

38. Ibid., 178.

39. Ibid., 187.

40. Ibid., 244.

41. Hans Urs von Balthasar, *The Last Act*, vol. 5 of *Theo-Drama: Theological Dramatic Theory* (trans. Graham Harrison; San Francisco: Ignatius Press, 1998).

42. Ibid., 270.

43. Ibid.

44. Ibid., 346.

45. Ibid., 351.

46. Ibid., 368.

5

JOHN A. T. ROBINSON, PANNENBERG, AND MOLTMANN: CONTEMPORARY PROTESTANT DIRECTIONS IN ESCHATOLOGY

John A. T. Robinson (1919–83)

Born of a scholarly Anglican family, John A. T. Robinson took his biblical and theological studies at Cambridge. After a period of pastoral work,
he became dean of Clare College and later of Trinity College, Cambridge.
He was consecrated bishop of Woolwich in 1959. Robinson's first book-
length publication was *In the End, God . . . : A Study of the Christian
Doctrine of the Last Things,* which was issued in 1950 and reissued in
1968.[1] He maintains that the entire Christian eschatological scheme was
simply handed on from generation to generation without comment.
He speculates that the possibility of the end of the world through
worldwide conflicts, disease, and the prospect of nuclear annihilation
has revived interest in the last things. Does the world have a purpose?
There must be some meaning and design to it all. Modern man cannot abide the possibility of a meaningless outcome.

If science is unable to disprove the existence of God, theology is also
incapable of demonstrating the existence of the Deity. Christ's own
conviction concerning a future life was grounded in his vivid experience of the living God. The New Testament does not ascribe to the
moment of death the powerful significance that it has possessed in
recent times. According to Robinson, the New Testament never clearly
affirms that after death there is no further chance for humankind.
"Indeed it could not do this without limiting quite intolerably the
inexhaustible love of God." He continues:

No Being who had an *infinite* concern for the salvation of
every soul could possibly be conceived as saying in effect:

"Unless you turn to Me by the age of seventy, or seven, or seven weeks (whatever it may be), I cannot give you a further chance." A God like that is either at the mercy of death, or He is not the God of the parable of the Prodigal.[2]

For Robinson this would assume a sub-Christian view of the father-hood of God.

Among the Hebrews, statements about the beginning and the end of things were couched in myth, since no persuasive evidence was available to them. The notion of temporal urgency is ever present in the New Testament, but that temporal urgency is actually rooted in moral urgency. Now is the time to decide and to convert. The culminating events in the life of Jesus were felt by the early Christians to be everything of significance that could ever happen, and hence they concluded that time must soon come to an end.[3] Belief in the second coming, however, grew out of the growing conviction that God's purpose had not yet been fully achieved. While the tradition of the Gospel of Mark assumes that future events will work their way to the final recapitulating event, the presentations of Matthew and Luke portray the last days as coming suddenly and unexpectedly.

From the time of the prophet Amos (ca. 750 B.C.), God was recognized by the Hebrews as the God of all history and of all nations. The early Hebrew notion of what happens after death was that somehow life goes on in a shadowy, bloodless fashion, which was not anticipated with much enthusiasm. This view was shared by many of the primitive cultures. Life after death came to be accepted as a pale extension of life on earth. In some parts of the world, the doctrine of reincarnation appeared, representing a welcome change from the endless futility of a shadowy existence beyond the grave. This prospect, however, lifts up an endless series of new identities and plays havoc with the perdurance of the individual. For Robinson, even the Platonists, who affirm that the spirit of each person is part of the eternal Divine Spirit and thus immortal, never really succeeded in establishing a personal and individuated immortality.

The Christian approach is quite different. We are not immortal by nature. It is God who calls us to a certain relationship with him, and it is God's Word spoken to us that opens us to an immortal future. Furthermore, resurrection is the ultimate destiny of every person. It was Paul who especially stressed the doctrine of the resurrection of the body. Robinson insists that the resurrection must be situated on the last day rather than immediately after the death of the individual.[4] He teaches that to speculate on the state of persons between death and resurrection is rather pointless, since we have no idea what actually occurs. Robinson describes the relationship between this body of ours and our body in the afterlife as one of nonidentity and yet continuity. It is this body of ours that is transformed, and not another. Otherwise, the continuity of our full, personal existence would not be preserved.[5]

Paul in 2 Corinthians 5:1–8 seems to be saying that our spiritual body is waiting for us at the moment of death. In 1 Corinthians 15:50–58, however, our risen bodies will appear only on the final day. Although Paul is largely concerned with the fate of Christians at the parousia, his observations can surely be applied to all of humankind. Robinson insists that the bodily resurrection will not occur until the last day.[6] The New Testament shows us two distinct pictures of the end time. John 3:17, for example, encourages us to anticipate the salvation of all, whereas verse 18 confirms the division between the saved and the lost. These two scenarios are not entirely compatible, but for Robinson they represent elements in the total Christian understanding of the end, and they must remain together.[7] The question of the reconciliation of these two anticipated outcomes has troubled theologians and Christians for centuries. Calvin's solution grounded in predestination dictates that all will be saved who are so destined, and others will be damned who are so destined. The second solution holds for the possibility that all may be saved. Robinson affirms that this position is almost unbiblical, although the New Testament declares that God will be, not may be, all in all through Christ. Further, the Scriptures attest that some persons shall, rather than may, be lost, so the dilemma remains. The classic third solution holds that God will be all in all in spite of the fact that a number of persons will be lost.[8] The so-called antecedent will of God desires that all will be saved, but the Deity's consequent will is that some should be damned because divine justice requires it. Robinson presents a more refined view regarding the salvation of all. Does universal salvation deny human liberty? Does the incalculable power of divine love negate our free will? Can we not imagine a love that would induce the surrender of all persons?[9] This kind of love would not disturb our freedom. Thus, he concludes that this approach to universalism would flow from the unimaginatively persuasive power of divine love and would not make us any less human or less free.[10]

Robinson discusses the incident in Luke 13:23–24, in which Jesus is asked whether only a few will be saved. He responds, "Strive to enter through the narrow door; for many, I tell you, will try to enter and will not be able." Jesus warns that all must take a stand regarding the fundamental choice that confronts us. It must be remembered that our destiny with or without Christ will result from our personal choice. Regarding the eternity of hell, Robinson reminds us that God's love could modify hell's duration. The person who chooses to reject God and be lost is still somehow contained within the "nevertheless" of divine love.[11] The individuals who decide to live under the domination of sin would be choosing the destiny of hell, but their decision does not in any way invalidate God's power to turn their lives in another direction. Love must inevitably win out, for "God is greater than our hearts" (1 John 3:20). Robinson assures us that "the incredible must happen because in Christ the incredible has happened. . . . Hell has been harrowed and none can finally make it their home."[12] "And I, when I am lifted up from the earth, will draw all people to myself" (John 12:32). Robinson concludes with this observation: "There can be no theme upon which the Church owes it to itself and to its Lord to work out its preaching more urgently and more thoroughly than its gospel of eschatology."[13]

Robinson's study *In the End, God . . .* was reissued in 1968 with the addition of two chapters. In the new chapter 1, he attempts to relate the death of God phenomenon, raging in the latter 1960s, to the subject of the last things. After briefly summarizing the impact of the death of God movement, he reminds us that God is the one who goes on before, and that is where we shall find him.[14] In Robinson's second new chapter, he assures his readers that regarding the last things, there is much we will never know. Earlier on he praised Teilhard de Chardin (1881–1955), whom he says formulated a fresh approach for our generation. We must take care not to make our hopes too small, or even our God too small.[15] We must expand the horizons of life and confront them with the freedom of a fully mature humanity. Robinson comments, "What happens to me after death I do not know, and precisely what happened to Christ's body after death I am prepared to leave open, without my conviction of his living presence being affected."[16] The gospel does not shift the center of faith and obedience to some other world, but it declares it inconceivable that life should be limited by the death either of the individual or of the race.[17]

Robinson's second eschatological study, *Jesus and His Coming,* was published in 1957, with a second edition issued in 1979. He insists that the sayings of Jesus in their original form contain no clear reference to a second coming but rather were later adapted to speak of it quite clearly.[18] The traditional eschatological scenario includes the day of the Lord (i.e., the end of days), the last judgment, the gathering of the elect, and the end of the world. The day of the Lord for Christians refers to the final consummation of all things in Christ. The final judgment and the gathering together of the elect were consistent elements in the expectations of the Jews. The end of the world was also considered part of the panorama of the end time.

The first mention of the parousia, or the return of Christ, is to be found in 1 Thessalonians 1:10, which dates from A.D. 50–51. Robinson claims that Paul does not refer to the parousia hope as part of the tradition that he himself received. Nor do the very early sermons in Acts make unambiguous references to the parousia. He therefore concludes that there is little evidence that the expectation of the parousia formed part of the early strata of the preaching of primitive Christianity.[19] Robinson affirms that Peter's sermon in Acts 2:17–36 does amount to a full eschatological presentation. There is reference to the Lord's great and glorious day (v. 20), and in Acts 3:21 Peter speaks of Jesus remaining in heaven until the time of the universal restoration announced by the prophets. However, for Robinson the parousia hope as set forth in the traditional Christian preaching is not in evidence in the earliest layers of the kerygma. He insists that Christ's own relation to the consummation and the final judgment does not imply that he will come again to earth.[20]

Although there is no doubt that the primitive church expected the return of Christ from heaven, "as far as his own words are concerned, there is nothing to suggest that he shared the expectation of a return in glory which the Church entertained and ascribed to him."[21] According to Robinson, there is nothing in Jesus' words to affirm that the Lord envisioned a second coming beyond the culmination of his earthly ministry. Nor did Jesus in any way suggest that his death would precipitate the end of history. As a matter of fact, he assumed that the disciples would have to carry on his mission without him. In Robinson's judgment, the doctrine of Christ's second coming developed in the community tradition between A.D. 30 and 50. In 1 Thessalonians the return of the Lord is clearly described as a descent from heaven.[22] The parousia hope included in the eschatological discourse of Mark 13 was in Robinson's judgment incorporated at a later stage. Actually, the narrative in Mark 13 could well owe its present shape to the church rather than to Jesus.[23]

There is, however, the statement in Mark 13:26 that calls for a second coming of Christ, but Robinson insists that no other verse in Mark requires a parousia in the final days.[24] Also, with the exception of Acts

1:1–11, no interval is assumed between Christ's resurrection and his ascension. The two events represent what Robinson terms "a single movement of exaltation by and to the right hand of God."[25] Further, "of some second eschatological moment, of another advent of Christ after an interval—of this we saw no evidence in the teaching of Jesus; of it we found no signs in the earliest preaching and creed of the Church."[26] For Robinson the application of the teaching of Jesus to a parousia event in the final days is "a purely editorial feature."[27] From the event of the resurrection, "the Christ comes in power to his own till all is finally subjected to that saving sovereignty which God has willed to accomplish through him."[28]

It is difficult to discover where the parousia hope came from, although it must have originated somehow from the mouth of Jesus. Robinson is convinced, however, that there is no evidence of this event in the earliest apostolic preaching.

> This preaching ends on the note that Jesus, vindicated by God as Lord and Christ from the moment of the resurrection, reigns henceforth till all his foes submit, and that in the Spirit he has poured forth the power by which this is to be accomplished. . . . But there is no hint of a second messianic event in history and no idea of the Christ coming again.[29]

This scenario is most thoroughly presented in chapter 2 of Acts. Although chapter 3 seems to allude to the second coming, Robinson is convinced that there is no clear statement here that Christ will return again.

The death and resurrection of Jesus constitutes *the* eschatological happening, and after these events the Messiah reigns at the right hand of the Father. For Robinson the doctrine of the two parousias—Christ's coming and then his return—was first clearly articulated by Justin (ca. 115-65) in his *Apologies* and his *Dialogue with Trypho*.[30] John's Gospel projects a single theological movement. The Synoptics on the other hand introduced the idea of a second coming, a second return. "There the moments of sitting at the right hand of God and of coming on the clouds of heaven begin to fall apart: in John they are inseparably one."[31] The Fourth Gospel portrays Christ's death, resurrection, and exaltation as a single culminating event.

Robinson insists, however, that in the Gospel of John there are more allusions to a future coming in Jesus' words than there are in Mark.[32]

> But on the lips of Jesus this language describes no second eschatological moment after an interval, but the consummation and

fruition of what is now being brought to fulfillment. In Mark, we have urged, this unitary conception was originally preserved but subsequently disrupted. In John it is never broken: no division is introduced between the different elements.[33]

For Robinson, the parousia consists in the indwelling of Christ with his disciples after the resurrection. The risen Lord will be with them always. The so-called second coming of Christ really amounts to an abiding presence with his believers until the end of time.

Wolfhart Pannenberg (1928–)

Born in Stettin, Germany, in 1928, Wolfhart Pannenberg did his theological studies at Göttingen, Basel, and Heidelberg. In 1961 he accepted a teaching appointment at the University of Mainz, and in 1968 moved to the University of Munich, where he taught until his retirement in 1993. The English translation of his popular study, *The Apostles' Creed,* appeared in 1972. Pannenberg clearly ties the resurrection of Jesus with the anticipation of the judgment and the final transformation of all created reality. He identifies the resurrection of humankind as a transformation so radical that nothing remains unchanged, and he points to the resurrection of Christ as the paradigm of the new life. The instances of resuscitation in the New Testament (Luke 7:11–17; John 11) were quite different, for the widow's son at Nain and Lazarus at Bethany had to die again, whereas the final resurrection will bring us to eternal life.

According to Pannenberg, both Jesus and Paul belonged to the same Jewish tradition regarding the nature of the risen life. In 1 Thessalonians Paul outlined the Christian notion of the experience of resurrection (4:13–5:11), which was promised to the righteous. This, however, for Pannenberg presupposes the truth of the general resurrection.[34] Humankind has always speculated about a future life, for life here seems so incomplete. Thus, belief in a life after death has been a constant dream for humans, probably from the beginning of conscious life. The Greeks held to the notion of the immortality of the soul, while the biblical tradition expresses the hope of resurrection, which seems more in tune with our contemporary understanding of human nature and preserves the unity of the physical and the spiritual that we view as indispensable to human life.[35]

Initially the death and resurrection of Christ were seen as the first stage of the end time, but after several decades the early church came to look upon these events as the anticipation of the final days, which would occur later. Although Pannenberg does not choose to investigate the various New Testament traditions of the Easter event, separating fact from legend, he does insist that all the events surrounding the resurrection of Jesus have a basis in historical fact and are by no means purely legendary. Pannenberg warns that the persistent controversies surrounding Jesus' resurrection should not be seen as obstacles to faith.[36] He adds that the separation in time of the resurrection and the ascension appeared much later (i.e., in the mid 80s) and can be observed most clearly in Luke.

According to Pannenberg, the combining of the last judgment with the events of the end time is found among the Persians as well as in Judaism. For the Jews the Son of man is to be the judge in the final days. In the Book of Ezekiel (2:1ff.), the term "Son of man" (or "mortal") appears as a single individual, while Daniel (7:13) identifies him as a symbol for the human character of the kingdom of God at the close of history.[37] The Son of man who ushers in the kingdom of the end time seems to be an individual in the Similitudes of Enoch (1 Enoch chaps. 37–71), which probably date from the first century A.D. Pannenberg attests that this Son of man was identified with Jesus by the early Christians who were expecting the return of Christ in judgment.[38] Although Jesus occasionally distinguished himself from the Son of man (e.g., Mark 8:38), the first-century Christians identified Christ with the Son of man who is to come. However, references to the Son of man faded in the second century. Psalm 110:1—so frequently quoted in the New Testament—is consistently applied to Jesus, who is seen to be sitting at the right hand of the Father in glory. The application of this verse to Christ presupposes that the primitive church expected him to come again as judge and king.[39]

Christians have traditionally joined the notions of immortality and resurrection. The resurrection of the dead was thought to occur to all of humankind at the end of world history. According to Pannenberg, the transition between death and the general resurrection at the end time was provided by the doctrine of the immortality of the soul, although the separated soul was not considered capable of sustaining a full human existence.[40] The unity of the soul and the body was always thought to be indispensable for full human life. The earliest professions of faith make clear the identity of the body before death and the body that is raised on the last day (1 Cor 15:42–49). However, "the continuity of our present life with the future life of the resurrection of the dead must not be sought in the linear sequence of time, but that it lies in the hiddenness of the eternal God, whose future is already present for our lives."[41]

Pannenberg notes that the life of the world to come is not to be envisioned as the eternal extension of this present life. Rather, it is to be seen as the endless expansion of the vertical dimension of our current existence. Along with the general resurrection of the dead at the end time, the last judgment of all humankind will also occur, as well as the full revelation of the final kingdom of God.[42] Thus, the ultimate destiny of each individual will be revealed, as well as the collective fulfillment of human history.

In volume 3 of his masterful *Systematic Theology,* published in English in 1998, Pannenberg presents his definitive treatment of the themes of eschatology. He attests that the message and the promise of the kingdom have played a relatively minor role over the centuries. John of Damascus (675–749) was the last of the Fathers to set out a full treatment of the subject, stressing the resurrection and the final judgment as the major topics. Medieval western theologians followed much the same pattern.[43] Pannenberg writes that according to the early Lutheran authors, the world was destined for destruction rather than a final transformation. Since the nineteenth century theologians generally have stressed the importance of anticipating the ultimate evolution of the cosmos as part of the final outcome of the last days. In the twentieth century Christian scholars have made much more of the discipline of eschatology, although the resurrection of the body has been consistently debated since the latter 1700s. Immanuel Kant argued that humans are not particularly interested in bringing their bodies with them into eternity, for they have never been especially fond of them in this life.[44]

Karl Barth awakened interest in the themes of eschatology after the carnage of World War I. There has been a growing awareness that the topics of eschatology are vitally important to our human self-understanding. The subject of the last things must deal initially with the issue of life after death for individuals, and then with the final consummation of the human family and the cosmos. With the Jewish people the salvation of individuals did not take center stage until after the seventh century B.C., and is featured in the prophets Jeremiah (31:30) and Ezekiel (18:4). After this the hope of life after death came into prominence and is emphasized in the Book of Daniel (12:2).[45] In Christian eschatology our fellowship with Christ constitutes the ground of our hope of eternal life, and that hope is to be brought to fulfillment through the agency of the Holy Spirit. The early Christians were convinced that the full realization of salvation was to be effected by the Holy Spirit.

Pannenberg affirms that belief in life after death was attested to from the Stone Age through the burial practices of the primitive cultures, for these rituals expressed a confidence, or at least a hope, in the afterlife. It was in the fifth and sixth centuries B.C. that both the Greeks and the Jews crystallized their beliefs in life after death.[46] However, in the nineteenth century both the resurrection and immortality were seriously called into question by many thinkers. Twentieth-century philosophers such as Martin Heidegger (1889–1976) and Jean Paul Sartre (1905–80) portrayed death as the end of human existence. From the first century Christians have believed in the existence of life after death. Whereas Paul and 1 Clement (ca. 96) refer only to the resurrection to life, Justin the Apologist (ca. 100–165) speaks of resurrection to salvation or to judgment.[47] Irenaeus (ca. 115–200) and Tertullian (ca. 160–220) taught that the soul is immortal, but Clement of Alexandria (ca. 150–215) was convinced that only the divine Spirit could immortalize the souls of humans. The teaching of Plato that the human soul passes through a number of incarnations was never accepted by the early church fathers.

According to the Christian tradition, after death the soul lives on and operates as the principle of continuity between this life and the future life.[48] Christians took over the notion of the immortality of the soul from the Greeks, but unlike in Greek thought, each soul was understood to be the informing principle of only one person. The pattern of each individual's corporeality is grounded in the soul, which assures the identity of the glorified body and the earthly body. Aquinas taught that each soul is the informing principle of a specific body, containing within it the pattern of this body.[49] As the separated soul lives on, Pannenberg asks whether it acquires new experiences during the so-called intermediate period between death and the general resurrection. This question for him remains open.

According to Pannenberg, the final consummation can mean fulfillment for some and eternal pain for others.[50] Further, it must be noted that our scientific knowledge of the cosmos does not substantiate the theory of the imminent end of the world as envisioned, for example, in Mark 13:32. Current scientific hypotheses do not provide for a scenario that looks to an imminent end of world history. Pannenberg urges us rather to deepen our comprehension of eternity and its relationship to time as best we can. The way in which time and eternity stand vis-à-vis one another remains the critical dilemma in eschatology that must be probed as thoroughly as possible. God's existence in eternity has no need of either recollection or expectation. The Deity enjoys the abiding *now* of his present. Whereas God experiences the totality of life always, we can only anticipate a totality of life in the future that will integrate the many moments of our existence into a unity.[51] One day we will ourselves make the transition from time to eternity. "What we do know is this: when he is revealed, we will be like him, for we will see him as he is" (1 John 3:2). For God all things that happen are in his eternal present. And it is only at the end of time that all who die in Christ will receive the totality of their existence.

Pannenberg advises that as we ponder the transition from time to eternity, we should begin with the notion of judgment, which, he says, is intimately linked with the relation between time and eternity. Paul admonishes us, "If what has been built on the foundation [of our lives] survives, the builder will receive a reward. If the work is burned up, the builder will suffer loss; the builder will be saved, but only as through fire" (1 Cor 3:14–15). It is not entirely clear what function Christ will have at the last judgment. Will he be the intercessor for the souls who stand before the judgment seat, or will he be the judge? If the Father is the judge, the gospel of Jesus seems to be the standard of judgment for all—believers and nonbelievers. Pannenberg speculates that the message of Jesus is the norm by which God judges even those who have never met Jesus, for all will be evaluated on the basis of the Beatitudes (Matt 5:3–11).

The advantage for Christians consists in the fact that they know that Jesus will be the standard or norm against which they will be judged. Whether we think of Christ as the judge or the standard of judgment virtually amounts to the same thing. After noting the principal references to purgatory in the Catholic tradition (Lyons II and Trent), Pannenberg asserts that it is uncertain whether the fact of an intermediate state between death and the last judgment is really part of the core of the purgatorial tradition. He is inclined toward considering the eschatological purifying fire as the intensive, searing presence of the Lord himself to the soul just after death. He does affirm, however, that the rather unambiguous statements in the New Testament concerning the destination of either heaven or hell do not allow us to rule out the possibility of eternal damnation for some.[52]

Pannenberg reminds us that the heavy use of metaphorical language in the tract on eschatology makes it clear that the themes under discussion are beyond human understanding. "But about that day or hour no one knows, neither the angels in heaven, nor the Son, but only the

Father. . . . And what I say to you I say to all: Keep awake" (Mark 13:32, 37). Pannenberg affirms that the Holy Spirit is the power of God who brings about our ultimate salvation. "If the Spirit of him who raised Jesus from the dead dwells in you, he who raised Christ from the dead will give life to your mortal bodies also through his Spirit that dwells in you" (Rom 8:11).

The glorious return of Christ will constitute the completion of the work of the Holy Spirit. The new life of those raised from the dead and the coming of the kingdom will form a consummate unity. Those who will experience resurrection will not in any way lose their individuality in the process of becoming members of the risen body of Christ. All will accept one another in their uniqueness and individuality and will complement one another perfectly. It is only the final consummation of all creation that will reveal "the definitive proof of God's existence and final clarification of his nature and his work."[53]

Finally, Pannenberg addresses the problem of theodicy, which can be defined as "the attempt to justify the goodness of God in the face of the manifold evil present in the world."[54] It was the sufferings of the just and the successes of the evil ones that precipitated the development of eschatology in Israel after the exile. The presence of sin and evil in the world can be traced back ultimately to the freedom with which humans are endowed. Pannenberg affirms that "permitting evil and its consequences is implied already in the independence of creatures in general. . . . Some degree of independence is an essential condition of the existence of the creature alongside the eternal being of God."[55]

> The verdict "very good" [Gen 1:31] does not apply simply to the world of creation in its state at any given time. It is true, rather, of the whole course of history in which God is present with his creatures in incursions of love that will finally lead it through the hazards and sufferings of finitude to participation in his glory.[56]

Jürgen Moltmann (1926–)

After completing his theological studies at the University of Göttingen, Jürgen Moltmann taught briefly at Wuppertal and Bonn before accepting a professorship at the University of Tübingen, where he remained from 1964 until his retirement in 1994. His widely acclaimed *Theology of Hope* was published in 1965, with the English translation appearing two years later.[57] Moltmann affirms that it was Johannes

Weiss (1863–1914), Albert Schweitzer (1875–1965), and Karl Barth (1886–1968) who placed renewed emphasis on the discipline of eschatology. Jesus was portrayed by Weiss and Schweitzer as already having one foot in the next world.[58] Moltmann emphasizes that the promises laid out in the Old and New Testaments must be studied in considerable detail. For Barth the heart of the matter is to be discovered in the utterings of God, who is the revealer, the act of revealing, and the revealed. The acts of divine revelation herald the coming of the eschaton.

According to Moltmann, the fundamental Old Testament idea is that history is what occurs between the promise and the fulfillment. The Greek approach is based on the notion of the epiphany of the eternal present. Their god is the god of Parmenides, for whom "movement was impossible and the whole of reality consisted of a single, motionless, and unchanging substance."[59] With the Hebrews, the concept of history was very different indeed. For them everything strains toward the future. The Old Testament promises direct us ever forward, and in the New Testament the risen Lord is constantly on the move toward his future.[60] The Christian believer is basically the one who hopes, grounding his or her future on the future of Christ.

God leads humankind to a future that is not an endless repetition of the present but rather a pilgrimage ever onward. Moltmann points out that the history of Israel is a history of movement toward the realization of the promises made to them by God. They were not bound into a mentality of cyclic recurrence like the Greeks, for they were always moving forward and on to new experiences and new revelations. "Even when the period of nomadic wanderings ended in Palestine, this mode of experiencing, remembering reality as history, still remained and characterized this people's peculiar relation to time."[61] Their whole life seemed to be in motion, with every fulfillment giving rise to another promise of something even greater.

The dynamic of promise and fulfillment is built into the very fabric of Israel's history. As a matter of fact, the God of the Jews is understood in terms of the Deity's historic faithfulness to the divine promises. In the ever-recurring dynamic of God's promises and their fulfillment, the Israelites actually came to know their God, and their hope grew out of God's historic faithfulness to the divine promises. Moltmann notes that "those promises and expectations are eschatological which are directed toward a historic future in the sense of the ultimate horizon."[62] The Old Testament prophets foretold the destruction of Israel and portrayed it as Yahweh's judgment on his wayward people. Furthermore, through the prophets, the peoples outside of Israel are taken up into the new divine promises of expanding life and hope.

The promises revealed in the New Testament grow out of the experiences of Jesus. Through the resurrection, Israel's God becomes the God of all humankind, and history is transposed in a dramatic manner toward the future. The God of Jesus becomes the God of all. Moltmann reminds us that the Christian experience can be taken in a noneschatological way "as the epiphany of the eternal present in the form of the dying and rising *Kurios* of the cultus."[63] This tendency was no doubt encouraged by the delay of the parousia, and thus the attitude of promise could be transposed into a present experience of redemption, which can be enacted over and over in Christian worship.[64] Moltmann prefers to call this an eschatology of glory, or an eschatology of eternal presence, both of which can lose sight of the critical importance of hope in the future.

According to Moltmann, Christian eschatology must be forward-looking and full of anticipation, because it is the study of the forward direction of resurrection leading us to mission. Our mind-set must be aimed toward the future. With the prophet Ezekiel (chap. 37) we must be confident that God will bring new life into dead bones. In 2 Peter we read, "In accordance with his promise, we wait for new heavens and a new earth, where righteousness is at home" (3:13). Moltmann insists that it is in the context of the fulfillment of his promises that God is truly manifested as Lord. The promises constitute the basis of our mission of love and concern for our world. The Christian must be animated by an abiding consciousness of mission to his or her world.[65]

> The Christian expectation is directed to no other than the Christ who has to come, but expects something new from him, something that has not yet happened so far: it awaits the fulfillment of the promised righteousness of God in all things, the fulfillment of the resurrection of the dead that is promised in his resurrection, the fulfillment of the lordship of the crucified one over all things that is promised in his exaltation.[66]

Moltmann reviews his perspective on the relation between history and eschatology. For the Greeks, history deals with the past. Their hearts were riveted on the unchanging and the fixed. For the Jews and the Christians, on the other hand, history holds out the promise of salvation. "We do not drift through history with our backs to the future and our gaze returning over and over again to the origin, but we stride confidently toward the promised future."⁶⁷ Christian preaching can be described as the proclamation of an eschatological event disclosing the lordship of Christ over the universe, which will set all of us free to experience the coming salvation in faith and in hope.

Moltmann repeats his thesis that the New Testament message shares with the Old Testament its radical directedness to the future, and with conversion always comes a deep sense of mission "to bring about the obedience of faith among all the Gentiles for the sake of his name, including yourselves [i.e., the Romans] who are called to belong to Jesus Christ" (Rom 1:5–6). Moltmann adds:

> We cannot turn our backs on the open horizons of modern history and return to perpetual orders and everlasting traditions, but we must take these horizons up to the eschatological horizon of the resurrection and thereby disclose to modern history its true historic character.⁶⁸

Thirty years after the publication of *Theology of Hope,* Jürgen Moltmann produced his full treatment of eschatology, *The Coming of God.*⁶⁹ He stresses in the introduction that the topic must deal with the salvation of the individual as well as the transformation of human society and of the cosmos. He declares that this topic has always been of special interest to him. Jesus is immediately identified as the apocalyptic proclaimer of the end time, which he views as catastrophic. His life and death are animated throughout by his eschatological expectations.⁷⁰ Moltmann feels that after Hiroshima and Chernobl, many are convinced that we are currently living in the end time. Whereas with Karl Barth there is a persistent expectation of the imminent coming of the final kingdom, Rudolf Bultmann insists that every passing moment holds out the possibility of being *the* eschatological moment when future time ends and eternal time begins. For Ernst Bloch (1885–1977) also, there was no hope for redemption from history. Rather, it is to be sought in the depths of the immediately experienced moment.⁷¹ Messianic thinking among the Hebrews changed profoundly after the destruction of Jerusalem in 587 B.C. The exilic and postexilic prophets portrayed this awesome event as God's judgment on Israel, and they promised a future event of salvation from God. The ground of salvation was shifted from the experienced past to the anticipated future.

When we turn to personal eschatology, the oldest idea in our tradition is the concept of the immortal soul. However, is the continuing existence of a disembodied mind, without brains or cerebral activity, really conceivable?[72] The idea of the immortality of the human soul took its origin with Plato, who taught that the existence of the soul after death corresponds to its preexistence inasmuch as the soul always existed and will never die. After its bodily sojourn, the soul for Plato returns home to the realm of the eternal divine ideas. This Greek philosopher identified what is essentially human with the soul. Although Ezekiel (chap. 37) and the little apocalypse of Isaiah (chaps. 24–27) allude to resurrection from the dead, the most unambiguous Old Testament statement of resurrection is found in the Book of Daniel (e.g., 12:2), in which the author declares that many of those who sleep shall awake to everlasting life.

Moltmann attests that for Paul the resurrection of the dead is a physical happening that affects the whole person (Rom 8:11). Our mortal existence will put on immortality and we will rise up into a whole new community.[73] Although Plato taught that the human soul is immortal because it is divine, for us Christians the human soul is not divine. In death the human spirit is indeed transformed from a limited life to an immortal life. The human soul retains its relationship with God even after death. According to Moltmann, the Synoptic Gospels did not develop a clear theology of death. It is Paul who left us abundant reflections on death, which for him is the necessary result of sin. In the Gospel of John we read that those who believe in Christ have already passed from death to life and will not come under judgment (5:24). Also, Jesus said, "Those who believe in me, even though they die, will live" (11:25). Further, the Book of Revelation promises that at the end, death will be thrown into the lake of fire along with the infernal dungeon of hell (20:14).

Augustine taught that Adam before he sinned enjoyed the real possibility of immortality, but after his sin this possibility was lost.[74] Protestant theologians in the nineteenth century, such as Schleiermacher, held that death is the natural and anticipated end of our finite existence and is not the result of sin. Had Adam and Eve not sinned, they would have experienced a natural death without fear or anxiety. Barth also taught that death is a natural phenomenon, for we have been created as finite beings. Moltmann adds that although the Yahwist's early history (Genesis 3) seems to affirm that death is a punishment resulting from disobedience, humankind is destined to die a natural death, for everything that is born someday dies. In his writings Moltmann has made much of the notion of structural sin, which humankind creates— economic and political structures that bring about the diminution and enslavement of countless human beings. He is convinced that in the third world natural death is a rare occurrence because of the pervasiveness of hunger, malnutrition, and disease.[75]

Moltmann points to part 2 of Dante's *The Divine Comedy* as one of the clearest expressions of purgatory as it was defined in the Middle Ages. He feels that the notion of purgatory seems to be incompatible with God's unconditional love. The Orthodox churches hold to the existence of an intermediate state in which departed souls can be liberated from the negative effects of sin, but this liberation is due solely to the divine mercy and not to any human suffering or intercession. They encourage thoughts for the dead but offer no Masses for that purpose. Luther and Calvin opposed the doctrine of purgatory because they were unable to accept the validity of works performed after death.

Martin Luther proposed the thesis of the soul's sleep after death:

> He [Luther] did not think anthropologically from here to there; he thought eschatologically from there to here: If the dead are raised by Christ "at the Last Day," they will know neither where they have been nor how long they were dead. "Therefore we shall suddenly rise on the Last Day, so that we know not how we entered into death, nor how we came through it."[76]

For Luther the time between a person's death and his or her entrance into God's eternal time is no more than an instant. After death persons enter into the new world of the resurrection, and the notion of purgatory becomes superfluous. The intermediate state is rather the time between Christ's resurrection and the general resurrection when Christ hands over the kingdom to the Father (1 Cor 15:28).

Moltmann teaches that although the dead are not yet risen, they are with Christ. This state is not a resurrection but only a being with Christ.[77] There is no need, according to Moltmann, to do anything toward the redemption of the departed souls, for they are already safe and hidden in his love. Regarding the dispatching of some unfortunates to hell, he insists that this is not at all compatible with God in light of his faithfulness to what he has brought into being. "Believers will appear with Christ at his parousia (Col. 3:4) and will reign with him in his kingdom."[78] But this is only the initial stage of the general resurrection of the dead, which extends to all of humankind. "It is an inclusive and universal hope for the life which overcomes death. It is true not only for Christians but for everything living that wants to live and has to die."[79]

Moltmann raises the issue of reincarnation, a popular belief among Hindus and Buddhists. He asserts that this position fails to safeguard the uniqueness and irreplaceable identity of each individual. According to the doctrine of karma, everything seems to be traced back to the life patterns of the prior incarnation or incarnations, thus blurring almost hopelessly the inalienable identity of each person. Thus, the Judeo-Christian tradition has consistently opposed it.

Moltmann then turns to the consideration of the universal expectation of the end time, for eternal life presupposes fellowship and rich communion with others. God has revealed himself as the one who not only awakens the dead but creates everything new. What must take place before the final days is the eradication of the many systems of domination prevailing in the world, as well as the liberation of the oppressed and the suffering. Before what Moltmann calls the great eschatological event, these liberating efforts must be undertaken. The most commonly held of all medieval eschatological hopes was the notion of the thousand-year empire when Christ and his followers would reign on earth before the last day. The expectation of the one-thousand-year empire has been termed millenarianism. Grounded in chapter 20 of the Book of Revelation, the martyrs who have been faithful to Christ will reign with him for a thousand years. After this, Satan and his minions will be loosed for a brief period. When the evil agents have been conquered by Christ and his followers, all will come to an end in the final divine judgment. In the Middle Ages this scenario was very widely proposed and preached. Luther was convinced that he was living in the end time. He thought that the struggle with the Antichrist (i.e., the pope) would soon be over and then the general resurrection and the final judgment would follow shortly. The Christian Roman Empire came to view itself as the universal kingdom of Christ. Patterned after the Roman emperors, absolutism became the hallmark of ecclesiastical polity, with the papal monarchy at the center. Vatican II (1962–65) sought to temper this somewhat but was not entirely successful.

A sign of the approaching end time can be seen in our age in the prospect of a potential nuclear holocaust. That has become a distinct possibility after Hiroshima in 1945. We are also facing the prospect of an ecological Armageddon, with our dying lakes and forests, the extinction of animal and plant species, and the undeniable depletion of the ozone layer.[80] As industrialization displaced the agrarian economy, capital was accumulated in the countries of Europe and North America. This change resulted in the eventual impoverishment of countless millions in the Southern Hemisphere who are now without many of the resources needed for their own economic development. With the near demise of socialism as a political option, we are faced with no alternative to democracy, which does not seem to be a viable prospect at present for many of the countries of the third world. Furthermore, the standard of living in North America, western Europe, and Japan simply cannot be extended over the entire globe without ecologically destroying the human race.[81]

Moltmann asks about the relevance of apocalyptic themes in our day. Although they are heavily emphasized in the later Old Testament prophets (Isaiah 24–27; Zechariah 12-14; Daniel 2, 7) and were also in evidence in the New Testament (Matthew 24; Mark 13; Luke 21; Revelation) with their emphasis on complete discontinuity vis-à-vis the previous course of history, the coming of Christ and the outpouring of the Spirit subordinated these apocalyptic ideas to the positive anticipation of the return of Christ.[82] It is time to emphasize the motif of joy because of God's coming righteousness.

Moltmann notes that the thesis of the eventual salvation of all was condemned in a local synod of Constantinople (543) as a heretical doctrine taught by Origen. The condemnation reads as follows: "If anyone declares or holds that the punishment of the demons and of condemned humans is only temporary, and will end some time in the future, or that there will be a restoration of those individuals at some future date, let him be anathema."[83] The Augsburg Confession of 1530 and the Second Helvetic Confession of 1566 both proclaimed the doctrine of the twofold outcome.[84] However, the statement of the universal salvation of all reappears in Protestant theology in the seventeenth and eighteenth centuries. More recently, Karl Barth insisted on the doctrine of universal salvation. Moltmann advises us, "If the double outcome of judgment is proclaimed, the question is then: why did God create human beings if he is going to damn most of them in the end, and why only redeem the least part of them?"[85]

Paul's observation in Ephesians 1:10 and the statement in Colossians 1:20 seem to hold out the possibility of the eventual salvation of all, while Matthew (e.g., chap. 25), Mark (9:47–48), and Luke (16:9–31) speak of the twofold outcome. Moltmann concludes: "Universal salvation and a double outcome of judgment are therefore both well attested biblically. So the decision for the one or the other cannot be made on the grounds of scripture."[86] And then there is the issue of the meaning of "eternal" (*aiónios*) in the above New Testament passages. For Moltmann the word *aiónios* does not mean the absolute eternity of God but rather refers to the irrevocability of the decision for belief or unbelief. He insists, "God *desires* to save everyone: that is the divine resolve; God *can* save everyone: that is his eternal and essential being; God *will* save everyone: that is the fulfillment of his resolve."[87]

For Moltmann, Christ's descent into hell lays the foundation for our confidence that nothing will be lost. Jesus has suffered the experience of hell for us, enduring those torments so that these tortures are no longer without hope of an end. Christ has in effect destroyed hell for us. His all-consuming and reconciling love has by no means brought forth "cheap grace." Rather, this favor springs out of the indescribable sufferings of Jesus. Moltmann concludes this section as follows:

> In the divine judgment all sinners, the wicked and the violent, the murderers and the children of Satan, the Devil and the fallen angels will be liberated and saved from their deadly perdition through transformation into their true created being, because God remains true to himself, and does not give up what he has once created and affirmed, or allow it to be lost.[88]

The question of cosmic eschatology has been approached over the years in different ways. From the earliest Fathers and Aquinas to current Catholic dogmatics, the universe is seen as undergoing a transformation into a new heaven and a new earth. The seventeenth-century Lutheran theologians preferred annihilation over transformation. After the last judgment, except for angels and humans, everything else was to be destroyed by fire. Most modern Lutheran theologians, however, have returned to the patristic and medieval hope for transformation, which apparently was Luther's own view.[89] The seventeenth-century Calvinist theologians preferred to anticipate the revitalization of the world rather than its annihilation. On the last day every soul is to be reunited with the body it possessed on earth, while all the circumstances of our creaturely existence will be radically changed.

Regarding the spatial relationship between God and creation, Moltmann asserts that by means of the space given by the Deity to the created universe, creation is granted a certain freedom of movement with regard to the Divine Being, and at the same time, the cosmos becomes a privileged dwelling for God. The destruction of Jerusalem in A.D. 70 was an extremely traumatic event for the first Christians because it deprived them of their home base, where they were awaiting the return of Christ. According to the Book of Revelation, a new Jerusalem is to become the dwelling place of God, while Babylon/Rome is designated as the residence of the demons. The new Jerusalem portrayed in

Revelation has no need of a temple because the whole city is to be filled with the presence of the risen Lord.

Moltmann is convinced that although God did not need humanity, he elected humankind as a covenant partner. They thus became mutually related and, in a sense, mutually dependent. As the world develops, God somehow assumes into Godself this wondrous expansion. The treatment of God by the English philosopher Alfred North Whitehead (1861–1947) is somewhat helpful here. The *primordial nature* of the Deity is the subject of all the divine potentialities, while God's *consequent nature* is affected by the developments in creation.

> In God's consequent nature every real event finds its permanent fulfillment because it remains in him eternally. . . . What has passed has not vanished but has become immortal in the perceiving consequent nature of God. . . . That is Whitehead's impressive doctrine about objective immortality. . . . [A]s far as his consequent nature is concerned, the process of reality really does make God ever richer. If God lets the world affect him, then with every day he experiences more of it and his consequent nature becomes ever wider and ever fuller. If a completion is arrived at, then God—as far as his consequent nature is concerned—is wider and richer than he was at the beginning.[90]

Moltmann closes with the image of the Shekinah as the vehicle of God's special, intensive presence among humankind. When we think of God in Trinitarian terms, the divine presence becomes even richer, for "the mutual relationships of the Trinity are so wide open that in them the whole world can find a wide space, and redemption and its own glorification."[91] The reason the cosmos will be ultimately transfigured will be due to the communication into it of God's divine plenitude.

Observations

In John A. T. Robinson's judgment, our immortality is not a natural quality but rather results from God's opening up for us an immortal future. He ponders the question of the salvation of all humankind and urges us to imagine a divine love that could well effect the reconciliation of one and all. Also, according to Robinson, God's love could certainly modify the eternity of hell. Finally, the earliest layers of the kerygma do not require that Christ will come again to earth. Beyond his abiding presence with believers to the end of time, there is no unambiguous warrant in that early material for anticipating his second coming.

For Wolfhart Pannenberg the transition between death and the general resurrection was supplied in the Christian tradition by the doctrine of the immortality of the human soul. However, the separated soul is hardly capable of sustaining a full human existence. The final judgment will not only determine the destiny of all humans but will reveal the full dimensions of God's final kingdom. Pannenberg asserts that the final consummation can mean fulfillment for some and eternal frustration for others. The eschatological purifying fire is likely to be experienced immediately after death and only then, through the intensive presence of the Lord at the moment of death. For Pannenberg this is the real essence of the purgatorial tradition.

Jürgen Moltmann explains that the persistent movement toward the future is embedded in the very fabric of the Judeo-Christian tradition. In the New Testament the God of Jesus becomes the God of all humankind. Christian eschatology is characterized by this forward motion leading us to mission, which involves the salvation of individuals and the transformation of human society and the cosmos. In death the human spirit is elevated from a limited life to an immortal life. For Moltmann the notion of purgatory seems to be incompatible with God's unconditional love. After death we enter into the new world of the resurrection where the existence of hell cannot be reconciled with God's creative love. Why would God have created certain human beings if he is going to damn many of them in the end? Christ's descent into hell lays the foundation of our confidence that nothing will be lost.

NOTES

1. John A. T. Robinson, *In the End, God . . . : A Study of the Christian Doctrine of the Last Things* (London: James Clarke, 1950); *In the End God* (New York: Harper & Row, 1968).
2. Robinson, *In the End, God . . .* , 33.
3. Ibid., 58.
4. Ibid., 89.
5. Ibid., 91.
6. Ibid., 96.
7. Ibid., 100.
8. Ibid., 102.
9. Ibid., 109–11.
10. Ibid., 114.

11. Ibid., 122.

12. Ibid.

13. Ibid., 128.

14. Robinson, *In the End God,* 14.

15. Ibid., 13.

16. Ibid., 24.

17. Ibid., 26.

18. John A. T. Robinson, *Jesus and His Coming* (2d ed.; Philadelphia: Westminster, 1979), 12.

19. Ibid., 29.

20. Ibid., 38.

21. Ibid., 57.

22. Ibid., 110.

23. Ibid., 121.

24. Ibid., 128–29.

25. Ibid., 134.

26. Ibid., 137.

27. Ibid., 138.

28. Ibid., 139.

29. Ibid., 143.

30. Ibid., 156.

31. Ibid., 168.

32. Ibid., 175. These references are as follows: John 14:3; 14:18; 14:28; 16:16; and 16:22.

33. Ibid., 176.

34. Wolfhart Pannenberg, *The Apostles' Creed* (trans. Margaret Kohl; Philadelphia: Westminster, 1972), 103.

35. Ibid., 106.

36. Ibid., 114.

37. Ibid., 118.

38. Ibid.

39. Ibid., 123.

40. Ibid., 171.

41. Ibid., 174.

42. Ibid., 175.

43. Wolfhart Pannenberg, *Systematic Theology* (vol. 3; trans. Geoffrey W. Bromiley; Grand Rapids: Eerdmans, 1998), 529.

44. Ibid., 534.

45. Ibid., 547.

46. Ibid., 556.

47. Ibid., 569.

48. Ibid., 575.
49. Ibid., 576.
50. Ibid., 585.
51. Ibid., 601.
52. Ibid., 620.
53. Ibid., 631.
54. Van A. Harvey, *A Handbook of Theological Terms* (New York: Macmillan, 1964), 236.
55. Pannenberg, *Systematic Theology,* 642.
56. Ibid., 645.
57. Jürgen Moltmann, *Theology of Hope* (trans. James W. Leitch; New York: Harper & Row, 1967).
58. Ibid., 38.
59. W. K. C. Guthrie, *The Greek Philosophers from Thales to Aristotle* (New York: Harper Torch Books, 1975), 48.
60. Moltmann, *Theology of Hope,* 87.
61. Ibid., 106.
62. Ibid., 125.
63. Ibid., 155.
64. Ibid., 158.
65. Ibid., 225.
66. Ibid., 229.
67. Ibid., 298.
68. Ibid., 303.
69. Jürgen Moltmann, *The Coming of God: Christian Eschatology* (trans. Margaret Kohl; Minneapolis: Fortress, 1996).
70. Ibid., 8.
71. Ibid., 32.
72. Ibid., 53.
73. Ibid., 70.
74. Ibid., 86.
75. Ibid., 95.
76. Ibid., 101.
77. Ibid., 105.
78. Ibid., 109.
79. Ibid., 110.
80. Ibid., 209.
81. Ibid., 225.
82. Ibid., 231.
83. H. Denzinger and A. Schönmetzer, *Enchiridion Symbolorum* (32d ed.; Freiburg: Herder, 1963), no. 411. English translation by author.

84. Moltmann, *Coming of God,* 237.

85. Ibid., 239.

86. Ibid., 243.

87. Ibid., 248.

88. Ibid., 255.

89. Ibid., 270.

90. Ibid., 331. See Alfred North Whitehead's *Process and Reality: An Essay in Cosmology* (corrected ed; ed. David Ray Griffin and Donald W. Sherburne; New York: The Free Press, 1978), chap. 3, 31–36.

91. Moltmann, *Coming of God,* 335.

6

MACQUARRIE, SUCHOCKI, AND HICK:
THREE DIVERGENT VOICES

John Macquarrie (1919–)

After receiving a Ph.D. at the University of Glasgow in 1954, John Macquarrie lectured at this university until 1962, when he accepted a position as professor of systematic theology at Union Theological in New York. From 1970 to his retirement in 1986, he was Lady Margaret Professor of Divinity at Oxford University. In 1978 his study *Christian Hope*, which set out his basic positions in eschatology, was published.[1]

Macquarrie begins with an extended philosophical discussion of hope, which he describes as a universal human phenomenon, coextensive with human life. He identifies hope as an attitude or position one takes toward experience. It is always vulnerable, for it can easily turn to fear. Its object is some worthy good that lies in the future, which is difficult but not impossible to attain (the definition of Thomas Aquinas). The attitude of hope generates a trusting mood toward one's environment and disposes one to positive courses of action.

Macquarrie asks whether hope requires a religious base and responds that this is not an easy question to answer. A total hope, however, does imply some religious understanding of the world. Also, there has been from earliest times a hope that has lifted humankind's eyes beyond death. Even the most primitive civilizations did not seem to accept death as a total annihilation. "[A] hope transcending death has been characteristic of man from the beginning, and has deepened and transformed in the light of growing knowledge and experience."[2] It seems that our humanity is so completely involved in the process of becoming that the goal of life stretches out beyond death. Humankind does indeed possess an abiding taste for the infinite. Macquarrie attests that "the fact that man appears to hope beyond death is itself a good reason for believing that he has an eternal destiny."[3]

We are then introduced to the topic of Israel's hope. Unlike that of many of their neighbors in the ancient world, Israel's view of history was not cyclical but linear and irreversible—moving toward the unknown future. Their history begins with Abraham, who traveled from Ur of the Chaldeans to a new home. The eventual exodus from Egypt began the pilgrimage to the land that God had promised them. Their hopes came to center on the advent of a king who would establish with them a formidable nation. Their hope was grounded in the covenant they had forged with God. With the destruction of Jerusalem and the Temple in the early sixth century B.C., hope for this ideal kingdom seemed to be out of the question. As Macquarrie views it, Israel's hope for the future turned into apocalyptic, with its awesome visions of the future. Their future then becomes God's future, independent of any human intervention and no longer continuous with Israel's present history. The Book of Daniel (mid-second century B.C.) began the tradition of apocalyptic literature for the Jews.

It was at this time that interest began to focus on the destiny of the individual rather than on the nation of Israel. Their central institutions had disappeared, and their hope for a great kingdom had all but vanished. According to the ancient Hebrew belief, death ended the life of the individual. Sheol promised only the most gruesome and shadowy existence for those whose earthly life had ended, and this existence was indeed cut off from God (Ps 88:4–7). On the occasion of the Maccabean Wars in the mid-second century B.C., a belief began to surface in some kind of fuller life after death, at least for the just who had suffered in the wars. The connection between God and the individual soul came to be seen as not severed by death, and hope in some kind of resurrection emerged.[4] This belief in the resurrection took hold among a good number of the Jews in the first century B.C. Although the Jewish conception of history was linear, an event like the exodus was celebrated annually at the Passover time. God's promises to Noah, Abraham, and David were eventually confirmed in a covenant, and the people were expected to do their part in order to receive the blessings God held out for them.

The vitality of the New Testament community can be witnessed especially in the letter to the Ephesians. Christ as our hope and the hope of Israel was transposed to an entirely new level by the resurrection. Macquarrie is of the mind that the most difficult item in the Christian creed is the second coming of Christ.[5] The first generation of believers was expecting his return within a very short time, and the parousia was included in the earliest professions of faith. Jesus is identified as the Suffering Servant, and his humble beginnings were emphasized everywhere. Macquarrie notes that Jesus was relatively powerless except for the power of love. Indeed, Karl Barth noted that for God it is just as natural to be lowly as it is to be lofty. Jesus has eliminated everything that pertained to a power Deity in the greatest revolution in values that has ever occurred.[6]

Macquarrie mentions that at Athens Paul received a cold reception from the citizenry when he preached to them concerning the resurrection. They scoffed and said, "We will hear you again about this" (Acts 17:32). Although the resurrection is a primary article of faith, it does remain difficult to accept. There is the report of the empty tomb, and, more important, there are the narratives about the appearances of the risen Christ. Paul's systematic account of the appearances in 1 Corinthians 15 is probably the most complete and the earliest of the reports of the event, dating only twenty years or so after Christ's resurrection. Macquarrie makes much of the fact that the apostles were not expecting the resurrection, but the underlying theme in the apparition narratives is the presence of God in the risen Jesus, and the presence of the Holy Spirit as the Spirit of Christ. This continues to be the current experience of the church, which in its preaching and sacramental life enjoys the presence of the risen Lord in much the same way that he was present to the first generation of disciples.

Macquarrie attests that the primary vulnerability in the positions of Moltmann and Pannenberg consists in the fact that they both seem to exclude the present experience of the risen Christ and the ability of that presence to shed light on the resurrection.[7] He insists that we meet Christ in the daily preaching of the church, as Bultmann asserts, and also in our sacramental experiences. These privileged contacts in word and sacrament give us a fuller and richer understanding of the mystery of the resurrection.

> To have faith in the resurrection of Christ . . . is not primarily assenting to the belief that at some date in the past Christ rose from the dead, but rather the present experience through Christ of a life that has been renewed and revivified, a life so closely merged into the life of God that the Christian knows it as eternal life.[8]

We must return again and again to Bultmann's insight, even though it does not contain the total meaning of the resurrection.

In Macquarrie's judgment, Jesus apparently expected that the Son of Man would be someone other than himself (Luke 12:8). However, the disciples identified Christ with the Son of Man whose imminent return they expected. In Matthew 10:32 Macquarrie insists that this identification is clear. Then when the risen Christ did not return as anticipated, the entire scenario had to be rethought, and the parousia was then positioned at the time of the last judgment (2 Pet 3:1–18). At the turn of the last century, Johannes Weiss (1863–1914) and Albert Schweitzer (1875–1965) revitalized the discipline of eschatology, insisting that all of Jesus' teaching was radically eschatological and that the assumptions of the nineteenth-century liberal theologians had missed the mark because they had effected an erroneous alliance between the gospel and the secular culture of the nineteenth century. After World War II, Karl Barth (1886–1968), in his important study *The Epistle to the Romans,* insisted that there is little continuity between Christian faith and modern culture, for God's Word, crashing down from above, is discontinuous with every human word and achievement.[9]

For Rudolf Bultmann (1884–1976) the eschatological themes in the New Testament are mythical and too far-fetched for modern believers. These ideas have to be rendered intelligible by transposing them into existential patterns. The eschatological events described in the Christian tradition do possess finality in terms of their importance, for they point to moments of ultimate and radical decision in the lives of persons. The truly crucial time is the present when a life decision is being called for. Macquarrie adds:

> Like Barth, Bultmann seems to think of the eschaton much more in terms of judgment and demand than of hope, and it seems questionable whether in any one of his writings he gives clear expression to a hope beyond death. Indeed, one might say that Bultmann's treatment of eschatology is the most thoroughgoing example of a realized eschatology. The last things seem to be brought wholly into the present.[10]

Unlike Bultmann, Moltmann and Pannenberg are unwilling to bring the eschatological themes into the present. They are adamant that these events remain projected into the future. Macquarrie, however, insists that Bultmann, through his realized eschatology, has actually tied the resurrection event into the "now" of our present experience. Moltmann and Pannenberg, on the other hand, stretch out their eschatological hopes to the events of the final days, the return of Christ, the general resurrection, and the transformation of the world, although we really do not have any idea as to what these wondrous events really involve. Even though they do emphasize and articulate a startling vision of the end time, Macquarrie warns that their projections of the final events can run the risk of falling back into mythology. Further, he is convinced that "Moltmann's attempts to relate Christian eschatology to future-oriented political and social movements in the modern world are lacking conviction."[11]

Macquarrie then proceeds to draft his own vision of what he calls the larger, the total hope. Perhaps we should be looking forward to the emergence of a new stage of existence. The image of the resurrection of the dead can be seen as a way of pointing to the next level of existence in the world.[12] This new horizon will result from the cooperation between God and humankind. The work of Teilhard de Chardin (1881–1955) is cited favorably by Macquarrie as an example of the effort to chart out what he terms "the next threshold of human emergence." Chardin's explanation of "hominization" and the journey toward "omega" points to a human community that is in some sense suprapersonal. Although Macquarrie feels that Chardin portrays the journey toward the omega point as inevitable and virtually predetermined, he thus underplays the influence of human fallibility in the process. However, the new omega point must be envisioned in some fashion as a social unity of unique proportions between Christ and his body, the final human eschatological community.

Macquarrie then turns his attention to the individual dimension of what he terms the next threshold of human emergence. He insists that this must include a role for all those who have perished along the way to the goal. He raises the question of life after death without the body.

> Human life seems to us to be so closely bound up with the body that we cannot envisage for it any reality when the body is dissolved. It is for this reason that I remarked that it is perhaps easier to see the possibility of a cosmic hope and to embrace it than to entertain a hope for the individual beyond death.[13]

There are for Macquarrie three possibilities for the individual after death. First, the immortal soul may go on without a body; for him, this scenario is quite improbable. Without sense perception, or a brain, or memory, there would be little chance for a continuous personal human identity. Also, how would it be possible for a disembodied soul to have meaningful contact with other persons? And without such contact with other persons, how could there be any human growth? Macquarrie concludes that the alternative of a disembodied soul is an extremely vulnerable hypothesis.[14]

The second traditional alternative regarding the viability of life after death hinges on the resurrection of the body. What Macquarrie terms "this crudely literal idea of resurrection" carries a number of inconsistencies as well. Is Paul's distinction between a physical body and a spiritual body merely confusing the issue? Macquarrie attests that now that matter is understood as a form of energy, one can conceive of the possibility of some type of body, "different from the body of flesh and blood but sufficiently continuous with it to carry on its experiences beyond death."[15] Therefore, the possibility of a resurrection body does remain viable. Macquarrie then lifts up a third possibility:

> Could we suppose then that our destiny as individuals is not to live on as immortal souls or to be provided with new bodies, but to be summed up or gathered up in the experience of God as the people we are or have been in our several segments of time and in our bodies?[16]

By means of a large panoramic mural revealing a great number of persons and a variety of activities that can be viewed in one gaze—such as Picasso's *Guernica* in the Prado at Madrid—Macquarrie gives us an example of how our lives can be captured in the experience of God. For him this is more than a passive, inert presence for these persons who participate in the very life of God. They would continue to experience an enrichment of their potentialities, while the limitations and deficiencies of their past would be healed.[17] Macquarrie cites 1 Peter 3:18–20, which relates Christ's descent into hell, preaching the gospel to the souls of the dead, as an instance of God's healing endeavors extending to those whose earthly lives have come to an end. "This is the truth that I have been trying to express in a more abstract language, the truth that God's atoning work can be retroactive and that even 'the spirits in prison' can be brought out of their dead frozen past to share in renewal and resurrection."[18] And further on, Macquarrie insists that "if God is the God of love revealed in Jesus Christ, then death will not wipe out his care for the persons he has created."[19]

In his study *In Search of Humanity*, published in 1985, Macquarrie presents a series of essays under the caption of philosophical anthropology. He speaks eloquently about the experience of death and also the process of dying (chap. 18). He does not agree with Jean-Paul Sartre (1905–80) that death erases all meaning from life.[20] On the other hand, Martin Heidegger (1889–1976) ascribes to death a positive role in that it circumscribes one's life and hence gives it a certain definable space within the time continuum, for "human life in time can have a meaning and unity only if there is an end to it."[21] Although death in chapter 3 of Genesis is depicted as a punishment for sin, Macquarrie holds that death is simply the consequence of human finitude rather than sin.

In chapter 19 of this later work, Macquarrie deals with the issue of hope, which he considers the agent of human transcendence for the individual and for society. He returns to the notion of total hope, which he describes as hope for nothing less than the whole human race. He explains:

> Christianity . . . expresses its eschatological hope in such expressions as the "kingdom of God," the "resurrection of the dead," the "second coming of Christ," expressions that do not convey any precise *conceptual* content, but which are not on that account meaningless, for they do point in a certain direction towards a fulfillment of humanity in terms derived from the teaching and career of Jesus Christ.[22]

According to Macquarrie, this total hope assures us that God is real and that this is a hope that extends beyond death. We humans have always been animated by such a hope.

Macquarrie then returns to the three options that may be open to humankind after death. Although there is a strong and almost universal conviction that human life continues on after death, the alternative of the immortality of the soul is fraught with a number of difficulties. For example, he reminds us again that the activities of the soul are related to the functions of the brain, and it is difficult to understand how a human soul could function without a body. Also, how could the human soul relate to other persons and to the physical world without a body?[23] Without relatedness, what would human existence be like?

The Judeo-Christian tradition, on the other hand, focuses on the resurrection of the body from Maccabean times. But, Macquarrie asks, is not this alternative quite as unrealistic as belief in the immortality of the separated soul? Even Paul's distinction between the spiritual or heavenly body and the physical or earthly body (1 Cor 15:35–40) leaves us puzzled as to what sort of continuity is involved here. The resurrection of the body in a way appears to be at least as improbable as belief in the immortality of the separated soul.[24] Therefore, Macquarrie offers a third solution:

> It is not that an immortal soul will go on living after death or that we shall be provided with new bodies in the future, but that the embodied lives we have lived here are eternally present to God as he embraces within himself the entire past of his creation. To be so embraced within the divine life would be the goal of human transcendence, which early writers ventured to call "deification."[25]

This hypothesis does not necessarily involve some sort of absorption into the Deity but can be seen as "the most intense communion, the final vision of God."[26] Macquarrie concludes by observing that the efforts to articulate the dimensions of hope beyond death are by necessity quite speculative.

Marjorie Hewitt Suchocki (1933–)

After serving as dean of Wesley Theological Seminary, Marjorie Suchocki moved on to the post of professor of theology at the Claremont Graduate School of Theology in Claremont, California. Since her retirement in 2002, she has become codirector for the Center of Process Studies at Claremont. She identifies herself as a disciple of Alfred North Whitehead (1861–1947) and Charles Hartshorne (1897–2000). In 1988 Suchocki published *The End of Evil*, subtitled *Process Eschatology in Historical Context*, which reveals her principal eschatological positions.[27] Although the purpose of the study is to probe the origin and the final resolution of the question of the existence of evil in the world, she does come to grips with a number of the classical questions relating to the last things.

Like many other scholars, Suchocki points to human freedom and finitude as the root sources of evil that are eventually to be overcome in what she refers to as the ultimate reconciliation of all things. Suchocki notes that while Augustine (354–430) considered all true evil in the world to be the result of sin, Gottfried Wilhelm von Leibniz (1646–1716) was convinced that finitude precipitated the evils in the world and in humankind. For Augustine the sufferings of sinners are part of the harmony of the created order, and it is the free will that is the radical source of evil. Suchocki maintains that in the seventeenth and eighteenth centuries, finitude replaced freedom as the more popular explanation of the pervasiveness of evil in society and in the world. For Leibniz evil was essential to the very nature of world harmony. In fact, for him the world is better off with the presence of evil than without it. He was convinced that as it is, this is the best of all possible worlds. While Augustine taught that there would ultimately be two cities—one for the saved and one for the damned—Leibniz held to the notion that both the saved and the damned would be incorporated into the one eternal city.[28] The only solution for the overcoming of evil was for him the final harmony wherein evil is assimilated into the good.

Suchocki then discusses the position of Immanuel Kant (1724–1804), who located evil solely in the freedom of the will. Jesus has provided the power of example for humans to overcome evil in their lives. Since his example is all we need to attain the goal of goodness, Kant consistently resisted the notion of grace. For Friedrich Schleiermacher (1768–1834) it is our God-consciousness that empowers us to overcome the evil in our lives, for it is the driving force in the creative evolution of the world. Suchocki discusses briefly the problem of the end of evil in Hegel (1770–1831) and Nietzsche (1844–1900) before concentrating her attention on Alfred North Whitehead. In her judgment, the process categories of Whitehead provide a more adequate foundation for the development of a unified theory of evil.[29] Whitehead affirms that because finite reality is dependent reality, it requires relationships for existence, and he locates the ground for each entity's highest good as God. The effect of God upon all entities is that the Deity provides an initial direction or aim for each actual entity, and this aim is proposed rather than imposed.[30] Each person possesses an inherent ability to follow the direction of this initial aim. For Whitehead self-creativity is fundamental to the process approach.

Suchocki then directs her attention to the issue of subjective immortality. It is her goal to establish the possibility both of subjective immortality and definitive redemption within the parameters of Whitehead's system.[31] For him there was only objective immortality, which means that every actual entity affects the entity succeeding it by means of the transmission of its own value to the other. Thus, not the actual entity itself but its perduring value is what continues in another. In other words, objective immortality is the passing entity's effect on the future.

In the Whiteheadian version, the *primordial* nature of God is God's grasp or vision of all conceivable possibilities for existence outside the Godhead. God's *consequent* nature includes all the actual entities who exist or have existed. Suchocki insists that entities can indeed be subjectively immortal in God.[32] That is, the subjectivity of an entity is everlastingly retained in God's consequent nature. The actual entity (or occasion) comes into being through its own self-creation and then through God's grasp of this self-creation. Although its temporal existence is fleeting, its divine birth in God's consequent nature is as everlasting as God.[33]

Each entity enjoys its own fulfillment and also God's consciousness of it in the divine subjectivity that is infinitely expanding. Furthermore, every entity included in God's consequent nature is expanded and intensified. The first experience of judgment, according to Suchocki, follows from God's reception of the entity that is assumed into the Deity.[34] For the process theologian or philosopher, each person is in a sense reborn moment by moment into God and is actually composed of the amalgam of all the actual instances of his or her living and that constitute the individual's earthly life. All the moments, all the wholeness of a person's life, not just the concluding moments, are present in God so that the individual transcends into the selfhood of God without losing its own identity. "Thus the essence of an occasion's [an actual identity's] union with God is its final bursting of the bonds of selfhood even while affirming that selfhood: the language is not paradoxical, for the reference is simply to a self, a value which is in its givingness, its relatedness to a whole which by far transcends it."[35] Each entity remains itself when assimilated into God's consequent nature, yet each is transformed. For Whitehead the final convergence of actual entities in God is described in terms of peace.

The ultimate fulfillment of every entity is achieved in and through its transformation in God, which occurs when it is brought into a relationship with all the other entities that have been assimilated into the divine subjectivity. The consciousness possessed by any assimilated entity becomes part of God's own consciousness.[36] Each entity so assimilated perceives itself in the divine being to the extent that it has realized its aim or destiny in life.

> Inasmuch as the consequent nature of God is everlastingly expanding, the whole to which the occasion [the assimilated entity] relates is everlastingly changing. . . . An occasion in God thus retains its own value, that which God has reenacted in bringing it again to birth, but experiences an everintensifying meaning to that value as it continuously feels its worth beyond itself.[37]

Suchocki attests that evil as well as good encounters the transforming power of God, and no one can predict the configuration of the harmony when the universe reaches its culmination at the end of history. The vision of Whitehead opens out to the deification of the world that is its ultimate redemption.

The consequent nature of God is continually assimilating the world into itself. (One should note that Whitehead did not rule out the possibility of successive worlds—one following after the other.) Suchocki reminds us that God's satisfaction is essentially communal. His intention for the universe is that it should mirror to the highest degree the Divinity's own nature. This reflection then becomes in a sense a privileged revelation of God in the world. And, Suchocki attests, "[T]he incarnation of God in the world is precisely the revelation of God as love within human community."[38] The evil resulting from the alienation of persons from one another is overcome as the mediation of the maturing community gradually draws persons together.

> Thus the satisfaction [fulfillment] of God is complete, since it is the fullness of all possibility and all actuality in transformative union, and yet demands further completion, manifesting itself in an everlasting transformation of reality after reality. It is a satisfaction which is in principle dynamic and unending; an enjoyment ever generating a moving intensity of its own actualization.[39]

The expansion of God consists in the transformation of the world within God's consequent nature until the world shares fully in the revelation of God's primordial vision of creation. This convergence brings about a mutual enhancement of both God and the world. Suchocki concludes that both freedom and finitude are involved in the universe according to the process vision, and evil is the outgrowth of both, flowing from the limitations of interdependent existence. Good and evil issue from the very fabric of our existence. God "everlastingly receives the world into the divine nature, transforming and unifying the world within the richness of the primordial vision."[40]

In her *God, Christ, Church,* first published in 1982, Suchocki refocuses her process vision of the culminating outcome.

> The reign of God places before us two destinies, blending into unity. On the ultimate level, there is the reign which is God,

our everliving and everlasting destiny. It does not now appear
what we shall be, but we shall nevertheless be transformed, reconciled with all creation in the depths of God in a justice that
is inexorable love. This destiny undergirds and empowers our
efforts for the second, which is the reign of God as it is anticipated in history.[41]

The same approach can be seen in the monograph "Spirit in and
through the World," which Suchocki contributed to the volume
Trinity in Process, published in 1997. She declares that the universe is
gradually taken up into the life of God within the divine consequent
nature. Furthermore, Suchocki proposes:

If God incorporates the world into Godself, and the world
contains conscious creatures, then God incorporates these
conscious creatures into the divine self. . . . The consciousnesses within the world are taken into the consciousness of
God—not to their absorption and disappearance, but to their
judgment, transformation, and salvation.[42]

The distinction between subjective and objective immortality has
resulted in much discussion over the years among process thinkers.
From the outset of her professional career, Suchocki has made considerable effort to emphasize the importance of subjective immortality
within the process scheme. The definition of objective immortality can
be stated rather simply. It is the quality whereby each actual entity,
when reaching its final stage of development, transmits its value to
another, and thus its value continues on and on. The question of subjective immortality, however, is more complicated, and some process
scholars reject the notion altogether, while others like Suchocki have
struggled to find a place for it. When God assimilates an actual entity
in transition, he also takes into Godself the *subjectivity* of that entity.
God also incorporates the evil dimensions of the entity in transition
and includes them in the divine synthesis, thus creating as much good
as the state of the world makes possible. Suchocki insists that God's
assimilation of each actual entity includes everything that belongs to
the entity assimilated. Thus, the entity *as subject* is taken into God's
consequent nature. If the conscious immediacy of the entity is indeed
fully retained in God, this constitutes subjective rather than objective
immortality. The subject then *as subject* is taken into God. This is how

Suchocki and others affirm and attest to the immortality of humans beyond death.[43]

John Hick (1922–)

In 1980 John Harwood Hick became the professor of the philosophy of religion at the Claremont Graduate School in California, and currently he is an emeritus professor at that institution. His principal work in the field of eschatology is *Death and Eternal Life*, originally published in 1976 and reissued with some additions in 1994.[44] Hick affirms that there were indications of the awareness of the existence of life after death in certain primitive human groups even before the Neanderthals and the Cro-Magnons. Stone Age men buried their dead with weapons and food that they might be nourished and protected beyond the grave. Some kind of afterlife was assumed by the earliest civilizations and often took the form of a descent into a lower world. It was difficult for the primitives to envision recently deceased persons as simply nonexistent.[45]

According to Hick, the earliest beliefs in rewards and punishments after death probably arose in Egypt, where the notions of judgment, heaven, and hell appear in some form. During the so-called axial period (800–200 B.C.) the idea of individual responsibility for one's deeds came to the fore in the ancient world, although the notions of punishment for the wicked and rewards for the virtuous were in evidence in Egypt many centuries before. Hick notes that among the Hebrews the prophet Jeremiah (ca. 626–587 B.C.) was the one who first clearly articulated the concept of individual responsibility for one's own actions. After the Babylonian conquest, faith in the continued existence of the Hebrew nation began to fade, and the individual became more aware of his or her destiny as a person.[46]

Hick attests that the idea of a blessed afterlife among the Greeks originated out of the mystery cults, and that the Dionysian cult of Pythagoras deeply influenced Plato. In his dialogue, *Phaedo,* Plato envisioned the soul as one's inner self that is essentially immortal, and he speculated that those who attain a closeness to the Eternal Reality find endless happiness. After he reviews the theologies of death of Heidegger and Sartre, Hick affirms that our thought processes are something more than phenomena of the physical brain.[47] The mind and the brain are independent of each other, but they do interrelate in a causal fashion.

In dealing with the subject of parapsychology, Hick suggests that this discipline does provide evidence for some concerning human survival after death. The consciousness of the individual acting as medium in a séance is replaced, in the judgment of some, by the consciousness of an individual who has died. Thus, this discipline urges that there is some evidence of human survival after death. According to John Hick, if we assume that the goal of human life is to effect and realize our human potential, this result is not often achieved within the space of an earthly lifetime. Forty percent of the people in the developing countries live in dire poverty, and many of them are devoured by disease or malnutrition before they can attain any significant degree of human maturation. Since this fact is undeniable, Hick looks into the possibility of some continued personal life after death. The only meaningful justification for the sufferings of humanity can be found in a life beyond death in which many or most of those injustices are remedied. This level of human suffering and misery would never provide an acceptable justification for the creation of the world without some type of a balancing of the scales in and through a continued existence after death.[48]

In Christian thought, Augustine's portrayal of heaven and hell dominated the western world for more than one thousand years. Hick insists that the image of the damned who are embodied and who burn everlastingly is as scientifically fantastic as it is morally revolting.[49] For him the endless torment of humans who have been destined to hell makes no sense at all. From the seventeenth century this belief has been questioned by growing numbers, and Hick observes that "the thought of such torment being deliberately inflicted by divine decree is totally incompatible with the idea of God as infinite love."[50] How could divine justice ever demand as a punishment for finite human sins an infinite penalty of eternal torture? In recent times a number of theologians have spoken of the lost souls as simply ceasing to exist after their earthly lives are over.

As Hick sees it, the majority of those who are to be saved are not ready to enter heaven immediately and hence are allotted a sojourn in something like a purgatory. However, the abuses that precipitated the Protestant Revolt—for example, indulgences and their sale—brought purgatory into a state of disrepute. Nevertheless, the idea of an intermediate state between death and the ultimate destiny of the saved seems to Hick unavoidable. He adds,

> I shall suggest that this function of "purgatory" is frustrated in official Catholic thought by the accompanying dogma of the

"final decision" at the moment of death, and needs to be expanded into the idea of a continued person-making process in other spheres beyond this world.[51]

The problem of heaven, in Hick's judgment, is to contemplate a meaningful human existence in which there are no needs, no deficiencies, and no challenges to be overcome. The essence of the life of the blessed is to be completely happy in the possession of the beatific vision, which Aquinas described as the enjoyment of the intellectual knowledge of the divine substance.

After discussing the positions of a number of modern theologians such as Moltmann and Pannenberg, Rahner and Boros, whom we have seen earlier in this study, Hick addresses the question of universal salvation and asks whether we are entitled to maintain such a position. He looks into the New Testament evidence and finds that there are two sets of sayings, a smaller group affirming the destiny of either eternal loss or eternal beatitude for all (e.g., Matt 25:31–46) and a larger group leaving the question of duration open. The Gospel of John (5:29) refers to eternal life and death, but the notion of eternal judgment and punishment is most prominent in Matthew. Hick speculates that it is uncertain whether Jesus meant that the punishment of evildoers is eternal.[52] Also, he feels that Paul finds himself on either side of this question.

Hick insists that we must believe that God seriously intends and promotes the salvation of all, although our freedom calls for the possibility of our refusing the divine graciousness. He comes to the conclusion, however, that divine omnipotence overrules the wayward wills of humankind.

> Everything depends on whether God can in fact carry his saving work to completion without undermining our status as autonomous finite persons. And I have already argued, on the basis of the Christian doctrine of the creation of our human nature, that we may properly believe that he can.[53]

Hick urges that we must believe in the ultimate salvation of all humankind because of God's saving love and power.

He notes that Paul is the chief proponent of the concept of the resurrection of the body. He suggests that "we can think of it as the divine creation in another space of an exact psycho-physical 'replica' of the deceased person."[54] There is for Hick a "full bodily similarity" between the individual before and after death. His or her risen life will simply proceed as the life of the person who has just died. The notion of reincarnation, which for the Hindus and the Buddhists is taken for granted, is not so popular a belief in the West. The fact that the great majority of humans have never experienced an environment in which they can reach their potential as persons constitutes one of the basic foundations for belief in reincarnation. "And on the western assumption that we have had no previous existence and have been brought into being *ab initio* in our present state of inequality, the human scene seems cruelly unfair."[55] According to the Hindu and Buddhist minds, each of us has lived before, and the circumstances of our present life are a direct result of our previous existence or existences.

The theory of reincarnation assumes that from life to life, from body to body, the consciousness of the individual carries over into the new life. Hick does not subscribe to the theory of reincarnation; it does not really solve the problem of the inequalities of birth and life conditions because these inequities are simply deferred beyond our view. Further, some type of memory link is seen as necessary to validate this theory from person to person, and this link has not been clearly demonstrated to the satisfaction of many. Although reincarnation has been professed in certain gnostic sects, it has always been rejected by mainline Christianity from the beginning. Hick attests that "the ideas of pre-existence and reincarnation were burning issues within the early church; but it does not mean that reincarnation was at any time accepted by the early church."[56] He notes that Origen's third-century teaching on the preexistence of the human soul did not fit the pattern of reincarnation because the preexisting soul did not exist on earth and did not form a part of a series of souls related one to the other.

Hick then turns to the reasons that reincarnation is irreconcilable with Christianity. First, it was not taught in the New Testament. It seems clear that neither Jesus nor the New Testament authors found the position acceptable. Nor is there patristic evidence of any sympathy for the notion. Finally, Christian teaching has always insisted on the critical importance of our present life as the exclusive period for determining our eternal destiny.[57] The Hindus and Buddhists feel that Christians are essentially unfair in insisting on what they call our western position. According to the Indian approach, human growth and fulfillment occur in and through the process of repeated successions of life on this planet. The ground for the continuity consists in the assertion that humans are psychophysical composites, such that life after death is realized in a body that expresses the "inner character" of the individual. Hick suggests that the once-and-for-all character of Jesus' passion and death could allow for the possibility of reincarnation in the Christian context, but he is not proposing any such modification of Christian theology.[58] Although he cites published cases of persons who seem to have had memories of a previous life, Hick affirms that most of these cases have not been scientifically evaluated and that many of them come from societies in Southeast Asia where reincarnation is a widely held belief. Therefore, he concludes that the theory of reincarnation has not been demonstrated.[59] One is left with the impression that John Hick is unable to arrive at a fully satisfying judgment concerning reincarnation. Although the position does address to some extent the unfairness of the conditions of human existence, it seems to lack an adequate demonstration to ground its credibility. Thus, the thesis is not especially convincing outside those cultures favorable to it.

According to Hick, the conscious ego will continue to exist after the person dies. However, not many will advance to their final state of self-realization immediately after death. Therefore, some "person-making purpose" must preserve us in being beyond this life so that we can achieve the relative fullness of our human potential. This fullness can be attained, in Hick's judgment, through a series of successive lives, perhaps in a number of worlds, but he warns that we cannot be sure how long an individual in this process would remain morally the same person.[60] Would it be possible, for example, for a twenty-first-century individual to retain his or her identity in a radically different environment, whether on earth or elsewhere, five hundred to one thousand years from now? On the other hand, he feels that "there seems no reason to think of the transition to the next world as involving the end of our present conscious self. . . . But these are questions which must remain unanswered in our present life."[61]

Whereas in the Hindu and Buddhist worlds human self-realization is charted out across an immense time frame, in the western cultures Hick speculates that the number of successive embodiments would be envisioned as very much less, although he cites no clear reason for the difference. He continues to insist that the future beyond death will be a genuine spatial-temporal environment, allowing for a real personal life including interactions with other people. There is no doubt that the eastern and western views of human existence beyond death are profoundly different from each other. Both approaches, however, can be envisioned only in the most general terms.

In his concluding section on the eschaton, Hick speculates that the evolution of personal individuality seems to amount to a transcending of it. The perfected personal centers "will have become mutually inclusive and open to one another in a richly complex shared consciousness. The barrier between their common unconscious life and their individual consciousnesses will have disappeared, so that they experience an intimacy of personal community which we can at present barely imagine."[62] Thus, individuals will become mutually inclusive in the context of a shared consciousness, which as Hick suggests, represents a model of the Christian Trinity. Each perfected person with his or her own center of consciousness will include others in a full total mutual communion of consciousnesses that will contribute to the collective consciousness of humankind. This concept resembles the Atman of Hindu thought.

> Our eschatological speculation terminates in the idea of the unity of mankind in a state in which the ego-aspect of individual consciousness has been left behind and the relational aspect has developed into a total community which is one-in-many and many-in-one, existing in a state which is probably not embodied and probably not in time.[63]

In a series of monographs published in 1993, Hick included a study entitled "A Possible Conception of Life after Death."[64] The need for a period of continued existence beyond our earthly life is again emphasized in order to allow the great numbers of humans to reach an adequate level of maturation. He asserts that probably 50 percent of the persons born in the past one hundred thousand years or so have died in infancy. Also, the circumstances into which humans are born may "vary so greatly in their propitiousness for moral and spiritual growth that it is hard to see how we could be fairly assessed in our performance in this one brief and chancy life."[65] Hick appreciates the value of the eastern option of a series of finite lives that end when we have achieved our final perfection and fulfillment. However, he does not agree that the case for reincarnation has been successfully argued. He concludes, "Let us, then, tentatively entertain the thought that having died in this world we are, either immediately or after an interval, born in another physical world in another space."[66] Although he is willing to grant that his thesis is very speculative, Hick suggests the following:

> At bodily death the empirical self, with its culture-bound personality and time-bound memories, gradually begins to fade away, our consciousness becoming centred in the moral/

spiritual attitudes which constitute the soul; and that soul, or dispositional structure, is then able to be embodied again to engage once more in the creative process.[67]

This period of development will continue, in Hick's hypothesis, as long as needed for the person to attain possession of his or her deeper self or soul.

Observations

John Macquarrie places great stress on hope as the ground of eschatology. Israel's hope for an earthly kingdom faded after the destruction of Jerusalem and the temple in the sixth century B.C., and emphasis shifted to the destiny of the individual. Sheol was then replaced by the prospect of some kind of life after death for the just. In the New Testament the resurrection of Jesus changed everything. All of humanity could then lift up its eyes to a future beyond death and to a new stage of existence. Macquarrie notes that life after death should involve a bodily component, for we could not relate to others without it. He actually prefers the idea of being gathered up into the experience of God, our inclusion into the divine life, as the most adequate explanation of our ultimate destiny after death.

The process view of eschatology is probed by Marjorie Hewitt Suchocki, who debates whether human freedom or human finitude is the true root of evil in the world. She attempts to establish the possibility of subjective immortality within the Whiteheadian system. For her this would amount to the subjectivity of an entity (or person after death) being retained in God's consequent nature, which is as everlasting as God. Each entity so assimilated perceives itself in the divine being to the extent that it has realized its aim or destiny in life. Evil as well as good encounter the transforming power of God, which will eventually effect the deification of the world. When God assimilates a being into Godself, he also takes into Godself the subjectivity of that being. Suchocki thus explains the immortality of humans beyond death.

John Hick introduces us into the very different world of Hindu and Buddhist thought regarding the afterlife and compares the eastern and western approaches. He is convinced that many, perhaps most people, are simply unable to attain any adequate degree of human maturation "within our brief and chancy life." Therefore, he explores the idea of reincarnation, which attracts him but does not convince him totally. Some extension of the process of human development for persons, allowing them to achieve a greater degree of human perfection, is for him imperative. He strongly rejects the notion of an eternal hell and eternal torment, for the prospect of endless torture for finite human sin is, in his estimate, morally revolting. Hick therefore holds out the need for an intermediate state after death and the importance of a "continued person-making process" perhaps in other spheres beyond this world. He strongly advocates the ultimate salvation of all.

NOTES

1. John Macquarrie, *Christian Hope* (New York: Seabury Press, 1978).
2. Ibid., 21.
3. Ibid., 26.
4. Ibid., 41.
5. Ibid., 58.
6. Ibid., 63.
7. Ibid., 76.
8. Ibid., 78.
9. Ibid., 99.
10. Ibid., 100–101.
11. Ibid., 103.
12. Ibid., 108.
13. Ibid., 112.
14. Ibid., 114
15. Ibid., 116.
16. Ibid., 118.
17. Ibid., 120.
18. Ibid., 122.
19. Ibid., 127.
20. John Macquarrie, *In Search of Humanity* (New York: Crossroad, 1985), 237.
21. Ibid., 238.
22. Ibid., 246.
23. Ibid., 250.
24. Ibid., 251.
25. Ibid., 252.
26. Ibid.
27. Marjorie Hewitt Suchocki, *The End of Evil: Process Eschatology in Historical Context* (Albany: State University of New York Press, 1988).

28. Ibid., 22.
29. Ibid., 62.
30. Ibid., 76.
31. Ibid., 82.
32. Ibid., 90.
33. Ibid., 96.
34. Ibid., 106.
35. Ibid., 110.
36. Ibid., 111.
37. Ibid., 112.
38. Ibid., 129.
39. Ibid., 142.
40. Ibid., 154.
41. Marjorie Hewitt Suchocki, *God, Christ, Church* (new rev. ed.; New York: Crossroad, 1989), 224.
42. Suchocki, "Spirit in and through the World," in *Trinity in Process* (ed. Joseph A. Bracken and Marjorie Hewitt Suchocki; New York: Continuum, 1997), 187.
43. Suchocki, "Charles Hartshorne and Subjective Immortality," *Process Studies* 21 (summer 1992): 118–22.
44. John Hick, *Death and Eternal Life* (Louisville, Ky.: Westminster John Knox, 1994).
45. Ibid., 58.
46. Ibid., 70.
47. Ibid., 119.
48. Ibid., 166.
49. Ibid., 199.
50. Ibid., 201.
51. Ibid., 202.
52. Ibid., 247.
53. Ibid., 258.
54. Ibid., 279.
55. Ibid., 301.
56. Ibid., 393.
57. Ibid., 369.
58. Ibid., 371–72.
59. Ibid., 375.
60. Ibid., 409.
61. Ibid., 418.
62. Ibid., 460.
63. Ibid., 464.

64. John Hick, *Disputed Questions in Theology and the Philosophy of Religion* (New Haven: Yale University Press, 1993), 183–96.
65. Ibid., 189.
66. Ibid., 192.
67. Ibid., 193.

7

FURTHER THOUGHTS ON ESCHATOLOGY: ORTHODOX, LIBERATIONIST, AND FEMINIST THEOLOGIANS

Orthodox

The Orthodox have traditionally given a triumphal and eschatological cast to their liturgies, especially their eucharistic celebrations. The doctrines of the second coming and the general judgment have never been subjects of detailed debate among Byzantine theologians. At the Councils of Lyons II (1274) and Florence (1439–45), though, the eastern delegates did enter into the debates regarding the question of purgatory, which they have always viewed as excessively legalistic. They object to the western insistence upon retribution for each and every sinful act, for they prefer to concentrate on the state of sinfulness rather than on the counting of each and every individual transgression. Theologian John Meyendorff insists that the Orthodox will never ascribe to a doctrine of indulgences.[1]

Neither the saved nor the condemned, according to the Orthodox, will attain their final destiny until the last day. Eastern Fathers such as Gregory of Nyssa (d. 395) and Maximus the Confessor (580–662) spoke frequently of the final communion and deification, but neither they nor the majority of the eastern theologians since have presumed to give detailed descriptions of the circumstances of life after death. However, they strongly affirm the resurrection of the flesh because humanity is essentially constituted of body and soul. Since Constantinople V (553) they have largely rejected the doctrine of *apokatástasis,* or universal salvation, for they feel that it attenuates our inalienable right to self-determination. According to Meyendorff, those who clearly reject the Lord's love will simply be destined to hell.

131

Sergius Bulgakov (1871–1944)

One of the theologians who made a notable contribution to the shaping of modern Orthodox theology was Sergius Bulgakov, who spent most of his life teaching at the St. Sergius Theological Institute in Paris. His only full-length study that appeared in English is *The Orthodox Church,* originally published in 1935 in London.[2] In the study he affirms that eschatology has taken on a somber tone in recent times. The Orthodox have always had a special reverence for the dead. As a matter of fact, the dead body is considered the seed of the resurrection to come and is treated as a relic. The separated soul enters into the world of incorporeal spirits, concerning which we know very little. Prayers for the dead are critical for the Orthodox because these intercessions can improve the condition of the souls of sinners and can lift them from their distress.

Bulgakov declares that there are two options for the souls after death, the beatitude of paradise or the state of suffering. He teaches that there are not sufficient biblical or doctrinal foundations for affirming a third place. No doubt a period of purification exists, but the Orthodox do not accept the western notion of purgatory. Bulgakov insists that the destiny of each soul beyond the tomb is completely unknown to us. Regarding the eternity of hell, he affirms several distinctive eastern ideas. For example, those who never belonged to the church or who have fallen away are not judged by the church and are left to the mercy of God.[3]

Although the last judgment will occasion the separation of the blessed from the evil ones, Bulgakov insists that doubts have always existed concerning the duration of hell's torments.[4] He reminds us that the doctrine of universal restoration was not only the contribution of Origen but also the teaching of Gregory of Nyssa, a venerable eastern doctor of the church, and these declarations of Gregory's have never been condemned. "Consequently they have the right to be quoted in the Church, at least as theological opinions."[5] Bulgakov mentions that although the Orthodox manuals of theology usually favor an opinion that approximates the rigor of Roman Catholicism concerning the eternity of hell's torments, a number of Orthodox theologians continue to adhere to the position of Gregory, favoring the final restoration of all. One day, Bulgakov notes, all of these discussions will eventually be settled.

Kallistos Ware (1934–)

A convert from Anglicanism in his twenties, Kallistos Ware, an Oxford mentor, is considered the most prominent mediator of Orthodox theology in the English-speaking world. In the first volume of the projected six volumes of his collected works, entitled *The Inner Kingdom,* he describes the notion of time.[6] For him time can have a certain ambivalence about it, for it can move either in a circle or in a relatively straight line, but the line can move upward or downward. The Christian view of time is that it is the occasion of God's favor (2 Cor 6:2). Time is the guarantee of our freedom, giving us creatures the opportunity to love. In the Book of Revelation, Jesus is portrayed as standing at the door knocking: "If you hear my voice and open the door, I will come in to you" (Rev 3:20). Respecting our freedom, Jesus gives us the time to respond to him in love.

Ware warns that regarding the issue of death and the hereafter, we must resist the temptation to say too much, for our knowledge is extremely limited. He insists that we must pray for the dead because we love them, and he declares that they will always be a part of our lives. We do not understand how our prayers affect the dead, but we are confident that they are beneficial. On the last day our bodies will rise again, and we will have the same body, released from the limitations of mortality, that is, a spiritual body. According to Gregory of Nyssa, it will possess the same form that the soul imprints on the different material constituents. "Whatever else can or cannot be said about the resurrection body, it will undoubtedly possess a transparence and vivacity, a lightness and sensitivity, of which at this moment we can form no more than a dim and totally inadequate notion."[7] Ware concludes his treatment of the risen body with the observation that we have perhaps said too much about these puzzling matters.

Ware treats in some detail the question of the salvation of all. He asks, "Could the blessed be happy knowing that some fellow humans have been plunged into the eternal pit of hell?" His response is that love could not endure that. God will never stop loving any of the creatures he has created. Yet if divine love will triumph over all, how are we humans free to choose? The New Testament passages dealing with the issue are ambivalent. Mark (9:43) and Matthew (25:41) threaten eternal punishment for the wicked, while Paul is inclined toward a more merciful position (1 Cor 15:22; Rom 11:32) and is confident that ultimately God will be "all in all" (1 Cor 15:28). Although the scriptural evidence is not clear, Ware is convinced that "God cannot be ultimately defeated."[8] His sovereign love for each person will in the end heal every infidelity.

The only credible motivation behind the punishment for sin is the reform of the sinner. The scales of justice do not call for infinite punishment for finite sin. However, unrequited transgressions do call for some kind of purgation or purgatory after death. The Orthodox tradition favoring the restoration of all is built on Gregory of Nyssa and theologians such as Isaac the Syrian (late seventh century), who taught that hell will not endure forever and that all will eventually be saved.[9] Although free will remains the strongest argument against universal salvation, Ware suggests that it is possible for those in torment—since they possess free will—to amend their ways. He concludes:

> [H]ow are we to bring into concord the two principles *God is love* and *Human beings are free*? For the time being we cannot do more than hold fast with equal firmness to both principles at once, while admitting that the manner of their ultimate harmonization remains a mystery beyond our present comprehension.[10]

Liberationists

The theology of liberation arose largely out of the pain and poverty of the third world, especially during the latter half of the twentieth century. Although there were strong voices that were raised out of Africa and Asia, the most notable contributors have come from Central and South America. Many have lately become convinced that God is indeed speaking out of the poor who in countless ways have been disenfranchised and rendered helpless by the massive industrialization that has occurred over the last two hundred years in Europe and North America. One of the basic liberation themes is that theology must not be relegated exclusively to the realm of theory, but must be translated into praxis. The leitmotif of the liberationists is the moving portrait of the final judgment set out in Matt 25:31–46. If Christians do not become involved in the alleviation of the plight of the disadvantaged, their religious allegiance is not authentic. God has expressed in Jesus a preferential option for the poor and the helpless. God sides with those left behind, and so must every believing Christian. The plight of the blacks and other minorities in the United States has also given rise to liberation movements.

Gustavo Gutiérrez (1928–)

Gustavo Gutiérrez has taught theology at the University of Lima in Peru for many years while living and working in Rimac, a notorious Lima slum. His study *A Theology of Liberation,* written in 1973 and revised in 1988, is probably the most important book published to date in the field of liberation theology.[11] He maintains that the Bible is fundamentally a book of promises and hope. The promises place revelation in an eschatological perspective. Eschatology should not be viewed as an appendix, only to be considered after the main theological themes. Rather, it should animate and inform the whole theological enterprise. This change of emphasis began at the close of the nineteenth century with Johannes Weiss and Albert Schweitzer.

Gutiérrez looks to the Old Testament prophets to set the mood regarding the future. The point of departure for the prophets was a profound awareness of a break with the past. The objects of their hope were largely very near at hand, although this did not rule out a transforming action of God at the end of history. Yahweh's self-identification, "I AM WHO I AM" (Exod 3:14), sets the scene for our orientation toward the future. The promise of the coming kingdom and the expectation of the parousia are historical realities that we look forward to here on earth.[12] The prophets proclaimed a kingdom of peace, but Gutiérrez insists that peace presupposes justice and freedom from oppression.

The "spiritualizing" of eschatology has made us forget or marginalize the pressing need to contribute to the coming of the kingdom by actively taking part in the efforts to transform the unjust social structures that enslave so many (Isa 65:21–25). The struggles for a just society constitute an indispensable part of the history of salvation. It is the "oppression-liberation axis" that reflects the heartbeat of the third world countries. The sins that the liberation movement chiefly attacks are the oppressive political and social structures. Gutiérrez affirms that "the salvation of Christ is a radical liberation from all misery, all despoliation, all alienation."[13] It is through the liberation of the poor and the disenfranchised that God's kingdom grows and matures on earth.

According to Gutiérrez, the process of liberation in Latin America springs out of a deep desire to create a new humanity, and this desire can be achieved most effectively through the promotion of justice in society. In fact, the development of a just society should constitute the new direction of eschatology, which must be based on urgent action in the present; such action will affect the quality of the end time. The point is not to interpret the world but to change it. Although Gutiérrez praises Jürgen Moltmann for his contributions in this area, he feels that Moltmann fails to ground his ideas sufficiently in the concrete historical experience of the poor.[14]

The life experience of Christ urges us on to the development of a qualitatively different society. "The Kingdom is realized in a society of fellowship and justice; and in turn, this realization opens up the promise and the hope of complete communion of all persons with God. The political is grafted into the eternal."[15] Gutiérrez points to Thomas More's *Utopia* as a model for the denunciation of the existing social structures. This vision of *Utopia* must direct us to the development of societal patterns that facilitate new and more mature relationships among persons. Gutiérrez affirms that faith "teaches us that every human act which is oriented toward the reconstruction of a more just society has value in terms of communion with God—in terms of salvation. Inversely it teaches that all injustice is a breach with God." He reminds us that "the Gospel does not provide a utopia for us; this is a human work."[16]

James H. Cone (1938–)

Many today are convinced that James H. Cone has been the animating force in the development of black liberation theology in the United States. He has taught at Union Theological Seminary in New York for roughly three decades. His study *God of the Oppressed,* published in 1975, represents his most developed theological position on the subject of black liberation.[17] Cone notes that he has been deeply influenced by such figures as Malcolm X and Eldridge Cleaver. As a matter of fact, he admits that Malcolm X has exercised a greater influence on his thought than Martin Luther King. King's teaching on nonviolence is not at all appealing to Cone.

Most of the work of James Cone is shot through with rage against the white culture and white religion. He identifies himself as black first, and everything else comes after that. He has succeeded in alienating many Christian theologians who happen to be white, in spite of the fact that he firmly attests that Jesus Christ is the point of departure for his theologizing.[18] He believes, however, that although Jesus is an important revelatory event, he is only one among many. "God speaks to people through many persons and events in a variety of ways."[19] Cone labels whites as the most violent race on earth, and thus their theologians are in no position to preach to black people concerning what they must do or avoid in order to be like Jesus. *A Black Theology of Liberation,* first published in 1970, outlines Cone's thought in the area of eschatology.[20] In the preface to the 1986 edition, he writes that his view of white theology is generally the same as it was in 1970, with the exception of a few qualifications.[21] For example, to combat sexism in our society, he has introduced more inclusive language. Also, he admits that he failed in the 1970 edition to incorporate a more global analysis of oppression to include the crises in the third world. In spite of these and a few other limitations, he agreed to publish a second edition with minimal changes from the original version.

According to Cone, God's call to the Hebrews was the result of their oppressed condition in Egypt, thus revealing Godself as the God of the oppressed. Throughout all of Israel's history, Yahweh was deeply concerned about the downtrodden. The New Testament also stresses the theme of liberation (Luke 4:18–19). For Cone the resurrection of Jesus means that all oppressed people everywhere become God's own people. He goes so far as to say that the only reason for the discipline of theology is to assist the oppressed in their liberation.[22] Further, he insists that there can be no theology of the gospel that does not arise out of an oppressed community. Cone asks, "What about others who suffer as much?" His response is rather obscure, for he implies that each oppressed community must generate its own approach to the particular crisis it experiences. He asserts that for blacks, whiteness is the symbol of the Antichrist. "In order to be Christian theology, white theology must cease to be *white* theology and become black theology by denying whiteness as an acceptable form of human existence, and affirming blackness as God's intention for humanity."[23]

Cone is convinced that the attempts to integrate blacks into white society have been a serious error, for the aim here is the destruction of black identity through assimilation. "Blacks know that there is only one possible authentic existence in this society, and that is to force a radical revolutionary confrontation with the structures of white power by saying yes to the essence of their blackness."[24] The promises concerning a future heaven, in Cone's judgment, are not in any way adequate to alleviate or soften the exquisite pain of black suffering.

Toward the end of *A Black Theology of Liberation,* Cone addresses the subject of eschatology. The significance of the discipline is dramatized by the certainty of death for all. He claims that blacks are forced to face up to the fact of finite existence more directly than whites because blacks can afford fewer bourgeois distractions due to their widespread poverty. The eschatological perspective has to be rooted firmly in the present, and this is accomplished when the oppressed say "no" to unfair and unjust treatment.

> To be sure, we may "walk in Jerusalem jus' like John" and "there may be a great camp meeting in the Promised Land," but we want to walk in *this* land—"the land of the free and the home of the brave." We want to know why Harlem cannot become Jerusalem and Chicago the Promised Land? What good are golden crowns, slippers, white robes, or even eternal life, if it means that we have to turn our backs on the pain and suffering of our own children?[25]

If the future is not realized in the present to some extent at least, what good are our eschatological dreams? If Christian hope does not somehow relate to our own liberation now, we may as well abandon it.

Eschatology therefore must be related to action and change now. If our thoughts on eschatology have no direct and meaningful relationship to the present, they are not important. Cone insists "that when Christians really believe in the resurrection of Christ and take seriously the promise revealed through him, they cannot be satisfied with the present world as it is."[26]

Then what about life after death? Once blacks were content with the prospect of a better life in the next world, but they no longer view life this way. "Heaven cannot mean accepting injustice of the present because we know we have a home over yonder."[27] Cone reminds us as follows:

> If we really believe that death is not the last word, then we can fight, risking death for human freedom, knowing that the ultimate destiny of humankind is in the hands of God who has called us into being. We do not have to worry about death if we know that it has been conquered and that as an enemy it has no efficacy. Christ's death and resurrection have set us free.[28]

James Cone affirms that black theology does not concern itself with detailed projections about life after death. Such dreams have led blacks in the past to stake everything on the life beyond, and they must not let that happen again.

Feminists

There is a growing conviction that women and the perspectives of women must be taken far more seriously in theology today. The notion that men can rule almost unchallenged in the religious arena has long been assumed in Christian churches. Further, the traditional exclusion of women from most ecclesiastical offices and ministries has deprived the church of the indispensable contribution that women can make in the life of the Christian community. A heavy emphasis on patrimony has narrowed the theological vision such that males have come to be looked upon as superior to females, whose subservient position can be seen not only in church organization but even in the formulation of doctrine. The female dimensions of God have been all but lost and must be reaffirmed, for otherwise we are neglecting fully half of the human equation, and thereby distorting it.

Rosemary Radford Ruether (1936–)

After teaching briefly at several institutions, Rosemary Radford Ruether became professor of theology at Garrett Evangelical Seminary in Evanston, Illinois. She remained there until 2003 when she accepted a position as professor of feminist theology at the Graduate Theological Union in Berkeley, California. To date her most widely praised book in the field of feminist theology is *Sexism and God-talk: Toward a Feminist Theology*, published in 1983.[29] For Ruether there are three principal varieties or strains of feminist liberation thought. The first variety, liberal feminism, fights against the exclusion of women from equal rights in the political sphere. Women must be given full access to higher education, equal pay for equal work, and equal opportunity to reach all levels of the major professions. Ruether also calls for women's right to reproductive self-determination. She is convinced that women have to work 50 percent harder to be equal to men because of the heavy domestic burdens they carry.

The second variety, socialist feminism, aims at the creation of economic autonomy for women. The fact that women usually have full-time second jobs at home frustrates their chances for significant advancement in the world of business and commerce. According to Ruether, the third direction of the feminist movement, radical feminism, focuses on the freeing of women from male control over their bodies, for this is seen as the very ground of patriarchy. Some of these radical feminists intend to reject men from their lives altogether, and this approach frequently leads to lesbian exclusivism. In this type of arrangement, the dominant divine symbol is the Great Mother. If men are included in this scenario, they must be satisfied with a subordinate place. This type of feminism is not acceptable to Ruether, for it readily becomes a caricature and isolates women from the wider society. What then is the sort of social organization that feminists propose?

> We seek a society that affirms the values of democratic partici-
> pation, of the equal value of all persons as the basis for their
> civil equality and their equal access to the educational and
> work opportunities of the society. But more, we seek a demo-
> cratic socialist society that dismantles sexist and class hierar-
> chies, that restores ownership and management of work to the
> base communities of workers themselves.[30]

Ruether suggests that there are two approaches to the development of this new society. Women can attempt to set up an alternative total community, organized and maintained by a feminist cell; however, this approach has many practical perils. The second option is the establishment of certain segments of society dedicated to the feminist approach within the larger community. For example, women could establish a system of child care units structured and operated according to a feminist design that will serve as the inspiration for other kinds of organizations dedicated to the same feminist ideals.

Although men and women are equal in terms of their finitude, Ruether claims that women are less concerned about their personal immortality. In her judgment males are more concerned with the mystery of death and what can be done to circumvent it. The basic experience of women is giving birth, and hence women are more involved in the support and development of life on earth. Ruether is convinced that our religious posture must be primarily focused on birth, the female birth experience, rather than on the male death experience.[31] "Why is this finite span regarded as insufficient for the boundaries of human life?"[32] Ruether suggests that it is probably due to the fact that we humans are able to conceive of a more favorable alternative to the life we have, but the ability to project other options does not make them real.

Ruether claims that Hebrew apocalyptic envisioned a limited time after death during which wrongs could be righted. This period of time does not amount to immortality, but it does constitute an interval after death when the injustices of this life can be rectified (Isa 65:17–24).

The New Testament Book of Revelation follows the pattern of later Jewish apocalyptic. The worthy Christians will arise and rule with Christ for a thousand years. At the end of that period, there will be a definitive battle with Satan and his minions, who will be overcome and then hurled into a lake of fire. The general resurrection and judgment will follow, with the wicked dispatched into hell and a new earth descending from the heavens. However, in the fabric of Jewish apocalyptic, even this final state is not clearly seen as lasting forever.

Ruether then centers her attention on personal eschatology. Is there some future life when the great numbers of what she terms "the toiling masses" are given an opportunity to restore meaning and depth to their lives? Her response is that we simply do not know.

> What we know is that death is the cessation of the life process that holds our organism together. Consciousness ceases and the organism itself gradually disintegrates. This consciousness is the interiority of that life process that holds the organism together. There is no reason to think of the two as separable, in the sense that one can exist without the other.[33]

At this juncture Ruether asks what will happen to us. She proposes:

> In effect, our existence ceases as individuated ego/organism and dissolves back into the cosmic matrix of matter/energy, from which new centers of the individuation arise. It is this matrix, rather than our individuated centers of being, that is "everlasting," that subsists underneath the coming to be and passing away of individuated beings and even planetary worlds. Acceptance of death, then, is acceptance of the finitude of our individuated centers of being, but also our identification with the larger matrix as our total self that contains us all.[34]

It is important for us, says Ruether, to transcend our individual conscious existences and to accept death "as the final relinquishment of individuated ego into the great matrix of being."[35] What she terms the final communal personhood is the Holy Being into which all our human successes and failures are somehow collected, although we are at a loss to comprehend this process. She concludes:

> It is not our calling to be concerned about the eternal meaning of our lives, and religion should not make this the focus of

its message. Our responsibility is to use our temporal life span to create a just and good community for our generation and for our children. It is in the hands of Holy Wisdom to forge out of our finite struggle truth and being for everlasting life.[36]

In a later work, Ruether blends her abiding interest in feminism with her approach to ecology.[37] She advocates exchanging a male transcendent Deity for an immanent female one, Gaia, the name for the Greek earth goddess, who should replace God as our center of worship. However, she admits that this replacement is not sufficient to solve what she terms "the god-problem."[38]

Elizabeth A. Johnson (1941–)

A distinguished professor of theology at Fordham University where she has taught since 1991, Elizabeth A. Johnson published her *Friends of God and Prophets: A Feminist Theological Reading of the Communion of Saints* in 1998.[39] In this study dealing with the ancient and venerable doctrine of the communion of saints, she addresses the traditional issues of eschatology. She notes that since the eschatological symbols are currently considered by many to be quite ambiguous, it becomes increasingly difficult to say anything concrete regarding our destiny after death. We simply do not know what is in store for us. Several of the key New Testament passages (e.g., Rom 8:24–25; 1 Cor 2:9) seem to discourage us from probing too deeply into the future.

In the Middle Ages the great repository of images relating to the end of days was pruned somewhat, and interest centered on death, judgment, heaven, hell, and the more recently explicated notion of purgatory. In our day, advances in science, psychology, and other disciplines have confused our traditional ideas of the last things with a cloud of unrealism. The dualism of body and soul and the relationship between the two have been studied by many who have raised doubts about how the soul could survive separately without the body. Johnson responds, however, that it is not unthinkable that the soul can endure separately.[40] Also, the notion of the resurrection of the body encounters problems in that bodies of earlier epochs are said to share many of their molecules with the bodies of succeeding epochs, so how could all of them be put back together again? Furthermore, modern science has many questions about the end of the world. What do we really mean by a new heaven and a new earth?

On the ethical side of the equation, growing numbers are convinced that interest in the afterlife has reduced our enthusiasm for the present life and for what we can do to improve the plight of the underprivileged. While the liberationists have dedicated themselves to the amelioration of the lot of the poor and the oppressed of the planet, the feminists have attacked patriarchy and the inexcusable subordination of women in many spheres of life. These recent developments have surfaced the need for a reinterpretation of the traditional symbols of the last things so that they can be weighted once again with new meaning.

Johnson alludes to the evolving concept of purgatory, which now seems to include the achieving of additional human fulfillment and integration as a possibility after our life on earth is over. Perhaps our final purification is realized the moment after our death through some sort of searing encounter with the Deity. The prospect of full and final maturation that would occur in the purgatorial experience is proposed by a number of theologians. Regarding the notion of heaven, the concept of a static and immobile happiness is difficult to comprehend, since it seems to eliminate growth and development, which are such essential dimensions of human existence. Johnson remarks, "Analogues in the human experiences of loving in freedom, enjoying beauty, pursuing truth, and interacting in community have an absorbing and life-giving character that is the opposite of stasis."[41]

It is the idea of hell, however, that is most deeply criticized in recent times as unworthy of God's boundless goodness. Johnson cites Schillebeeckx, who expresses amazement that people could accept the fact that next to heaven there is a place called hell wherein individuals are suffering the most excruciating pain and torment everlastingly.[42] How could the infinite mercy of God allow something like this to occur? Schillebeeckx has suggested that the definitively obdurate, if there are such, will simply cease to exist after their earthly life and not be submitted to an eternity of torture. Moreover, is anyone really certain that any one individual has actually been condemned to hell? The prospect of the universal salvation of all has been offered as a hope and as a possibility for humankind. Johnson also sympathizes with Rahner's idea that when the soul leaves the body in death, it is freed to become pancosmic, that is, more deeply related to the ground of the world. This proposal of Rahner's is appraised by Johnson as "not totally inconceivable."[43]

Three distinct scenarios are then put before us in the effort to transpose the eschatological events into a new context. For what she terms the recycling scenario, Johnson references the work of Rosemary Radford Ruether, who has challenged the notion of an eternal future for individual humans. Ruether feels that we must concentrate on our present responsibilities for the world, which are only diluted by our pre-occupation with a future existence beyond.[44] Ruether considers that the concern for individual immortality is actually a symptom of the masculine effort to conquer mortality. She urges that we abandon our individual egos and look to the great Matrix of being, the total self that contains all of us. Johnson urges that even for feminists the abandonment of our individuated futures is not the answer.

The second approach, the fruition scenario, in Johnson's view, mirrors Rahner's position that the passage through death amounts to a validation of each human existence by God.[45] How can we assume that at death everything is over?

> What has transpired during a person's history does not vanish into nothingness as if the person went extinct, but neither does it continue on in another time-like state. Rather, as an intrinsic moment in death itself, persons sum themselves up in a free self-affirmation, a radical endorsement of their lives' fundamental option, and so come to completion in God.[46]

Rahner's perspective, endorsed by Johnson, is that we are simply unable to envision the life after death. Those who are redeemed are "enfolded into the incomprehensible mystery of the living God."[47]

The third approach described by Johnson is the dissolution scenario, which offers us nothing but a leap into the future. We have no idea what lies beyond the portal of death, but we are hopeful and trusting regarding our destiny. Does God want everyone to recede back into the great undifferentiated cosmos, having created the world, having raised Jesus from the dead, and having communicated the divine life to us in grace? It is Johnson's firm conviction that the same gracious divine ways of acting will prevail in the future.[48] This, she repeats, is by no means an unreasonable hope.

> Because each unique life does not just sink into the emptiness of the void or merge with the All, then we do not simply acknowledge them as those who have lived and made possible our own history. Instead, trust in the Creator Spirit who keeps faith with the creature gives rise to the hope that the dead, whether famous or unknown, whether distant in time or our own beloved ones, are enfolded into the absolute mystery of

the gracious, compassionate being of God which to us is darkness but which to them is the fulfillment of their lives in the sphere of the Spirit. Their destiny signals the future toward which we the living are headed.[49]

Johnson affirms that the worthy dead abide in God. They have not descended into nothingness but have entered into the welcoming arms of God. Nor is the world tumbling toward nothingness. Rather, it moves inexorably toward its full and final transfiguration.

Observations

It is clear that the Orthodox have enriched the Christian vision of eschatology by keeping open within their tradition the prospect of the ultimate salvation of all persons. The liberationists have forced us to hasten the coming of the Lord's kingdom. The major contribution of the feminists is to insist that the subordination of women in the churches and in society at large is destructive to both men and women, thus frustrating the maturation of both sexes and the final fulfillment of the human family.

NOTES

1. John Meyendorff, *Byzantine Theology* (2d ed.; New York: Fordham University Press, 1987), 221.
2. Sergius Bulgakov, *The Orthodox Church* (translation revised by Lydia Kesich; Crestwood, N.Y.: St. Vladimir's Seminary Press, 1988).
3. Ibid., 183.
4. Ibid., 185.
5. Ibid.
6. Kallistos Ware, *The Inner Kingdom*, vol. 1 of *The Collected Works* (Crestwood, N.Y.: St. Vladimir's Seminary Press, 2000).
7. Ibid., 40.
8. Ibid., 197.
9. Ibid., 207–9.
10. Ibid., 214.
11. Gustavo Gutiérrez, *A Theology of Liberation: History, Politics, and Salvation* (rev. ed.; trans. and ed. Caridad Inda and John Eagleson; Maryknoll, N.Y.: Orbis Books, 1988).
12. Ibid., 97.
13. Ibid., 104.
14. Ibid., 124.

15. Ibid., 135.
16. Ibid., 139.
17. James H. Cone, *God of the Oppressed* (rev. ed.; Maryknoll, N.Y.: Orbis Books, 1997).
18. Ibid., xiii.
19. Ibid., xiv.
20. James H. Cone, *A Black Theology of Liberation* (2d ed.; Maryknoll, N.Y.: Orbis Books, 1986).
21. Ibid., xvii.
22. Ibid., 4.
23. Ibid., 9.
24. Ibid., 15.
25. Ibid., 137.
26. Ibid., 140.
27. Ibid., 141.
28. Ibid.
29. Rosemary Radford Ruether, *Sexism and God-talk: Toward a Feminist Theology* (Boston: Beacon Press, 1983).
30. Ibid., 232.
31. Ibid., 236.
32. Ibid., 237.
33. Ibid., 257.
34. Ibid.
35. Ibid., 258.
36. Ibid.
37. Rosemary Radford Ruether, *Gaia and God: An Ecofeminist Theology of Earth Healing* (San Francisco: HarperSanFrancisco, 1992).
38. Ibid., 4.
39. Elizabeth A. Johnson, *Friends of God and Prophets: A Feminist Theological Reading of the Communion of Saints* (New York: Continuum, 1998).
40. Ibid., 184.
41. Ibid., 190.
42. Ibid., 191.
43. Ibid., 193.
44. Ibid., 196.
45. Ibid., 198.
46. Ibid., 199.
47. Ibid.
48. Ibid., 213.
49. Ibid., 214.

AFTERWORD

The theologians reviewed here have raised a great number of questions that have prompted a considerable range of responses. In the New Testament, does the word "eternal" signify forever or a long time? Are those who spurn the love of God dispatched into hell, or do they simply perish? Is the process of expiation after death to prepare us for the divine presence a momentary experience, or does it delay one's entrance into heaven for a period? Does the soul after death retain an individuated life of its own, or are we merely absorbed somehow into the divine Matrix? Is the thesis of the final salvation of all a viable option? Is it conceivable that a gracious God would punish a single, finite, unrequited sin with an endless eternity of torment? Would a consistently loving God leave anyone along the roadside without showering on him or her the full convincing warmth of the divine affection? And how could one ever resist that?

All of these issues are hardly insignificant or marginal for believing Christians, yet they have brought forth very differing responses from recent Christian theologians. I hope these questions and the responses offered have allowed you to probe your own faith, remembering Paul's admonition that above all else we must hope for what we do not see and wait for it with patience (Rom 8:24–25).

BIBLIOGRAPHY

Adams, James Luther, Wilhelm Pauck, and Roger Lincoln Shinn, eds. *The Thought of Paul Tillich.* San Francisco: Harper & Row, 1985.

Alberigo, Giuseppe, et al. *Decrees of the Ecumenical Councils.* Vol. 1. Edited by N. Tanner. Washington, D.C.: Georgetown University Press, 1990.

Altaner, Berthold. *Patrology.* Translated by Hilda C. Graef. New York: Herder & Herder, 1960.

Althaus, Paul. *The Theology of Martin Luther.* Translated by Robert C. Schultz. Philadelphia: Fortress, 1966.

Augustine. *The City of God.* Translated by Marcus Dods. New York: Random House, 1950.

Balthasar, Hans Urs von. *Dare We Hope "That All Men Be Saved"?* Translated by David Kipp and Lothar Krauth. San Francisco: Ignatius Press, 1988.

———. *The Last Act.* Vol. 5 of *Theo-Drama: Theological Dramatic Theory.* Translated by Graham Harrison. San Francisco: Ignatius Press, 1998.

Bauckham, Richard, and Trevor Hart. *Hope against Hope: Christian Eschatology at the Turn of the Millennium.* Grand Rapids: Eerdmans, 1999.

Boadt, Lawrence. *Reading the Old Testament.* New York: Paulist Press, 1984.

Boff, Leonardo. *Jesus Christ Liberator.* Translated by Patrick Hughes. Maryknoll, N.Y.: Orbis Books, 1978; repr. 1991.

Boismard, Marie-Emile. *Our Victory over Death: Resurrection?* Translated by Madeleine Beaumont. Collegeville, Minn.: Liturgical Press, 1999.

Boros, Ladislaus. "Has Life a Meaning?" Translated by John Griffiths. *Concilium* 60 (1970): 11–20.

————. *Living in Hope.* Translated by W. J. O'Hara. New York: Herder & Herder, 1968.

————. *The Moment of Truth: Mysterium Mortis.* Translated by Gregory Bainbridge. London: Burns & Oates, 1965.

————. *We Are Future.* Translated by W. J. O'Hara. New York: Herder & Herder, 1970.

Bouwsma, William J. *John Calvin: A Sixteenth-Century Portrait.* New York: Oxford University Press, 1988.

Bulgakov, Sergius. *The Orthodox Church.* Translation revised by Lydia Kesich. Crestwood, N.Y.: St. Vladimir's Seminary Press, 1988.

Bultmann, Rudolf. *Faith and Understanding.* Translated by Louise Pettibone Smith. Philadelphia: Fortress, 1987.

————. *History and Eschatology: The Presence of Eternity.* New York: Harper & Row, 1957.

————. *The History of the Synoptic Tradition.* Rev. ed. Translated by John Marsh. Peabody, Mass.: Hendrickson, 1963.

————. *Jesus Christ and Mythology.* New York: Scribner's, 1958.

————. *Jesus and the Word.* Translated by Louise Smith and Erminie Lantero. New York: Scribner's, 1958.

————. *Theology of the New Testament.* 2 vols. Translated by Kendrick Grobel. London: SCM Press, 1952, 1955.

Calvin's Institutes: A New Compend. Edited by Hugh T. Kerr. Louisville, Ky.: Westminster John Knox, 1989.

Cassirer, Ernst. *The Philosophy of the Enlightenment.* Translated by Fritz C. A. Koelln and James P. Pettegrove. Princeton: Princeton University Press, 1951; repr. 1979.

Clements, Keith W. *Friedrich Schleiermacher: Pioneer of Modern Theology.* London: Collins Liturgical Publications, 1987.

Cone, James H. *A Black Theology of Liberation.* 2d ed. Maryknoll, N.Y.: Orbis Books, 1986.

————. *God of the Oppressed.* Rev. ed. Maryknoll, N.Y.: Orbis Books, 1997.

Copleston, Frederick. *A History of Philosophy.* Vols. 4–6. 1st ed. 1963–64. Repr., Garden City, N.Y.: Image Books, 1985.

Cullmann, Oscar. *Christ and Time.* Rev. ed. Translated by Floyd F. Filson. London: SCM Press, 1962.

————. *Immortality of the Soul or Resurrection of the Dead? The Witness of the New Testament.* London: Epworth Press, 1958.

————. *Salvation in History.* Translated by Sidney G. Sowers. New York: Harper & Row, 1967.

Daley, Brian E. *The Hope of the Early Church: A Handbook of Patristic Eschatology.* Cambridge: Cambridge University Press, 1991.

Denzinger, H., and A. Schönmetzer. *Enchiridion Symbolorum.* 32d ed. Freiburg: Herder, 1963.

Dubarle, André-Marie. "Belief in Immortality in the Old Testament and Judaism." *Concilium* 66 (1970): 34–45.

Dunn, James D. G. *The Theology of Paul the Apostle.* Grand Rapids: Eerdmans, 1998.

———. *Unity and Diversity in the New Testament.* 2d ed. London: SCM Press, 1990.

Gay, Peter. *The Enlightenment: The Rise of Modern Paganism.* New York: W. W. Norton, 1966.

Grant, Robert M. *Irenaeus of Lyons.* New York: Routledge, 1997.

Gregory of Nyssa. *On the Soul and the Resurrection.* Translated by Catharine P. Roth. Crestwood, N.Y.: St. Vladimir's Seminary Press, 1993.

Grillmeier, Aloys, and Theresia Hainthaler. *Christ in Christian Tradition.* Vol. 2, pt. 2. Translated by Pauline Allen and John Cawte. Louisville, Ky.: Westminster John Knox, 1955.

Gutiérrez, Gustavo. *Gustavo Gutiérrez: Essential Writings.* Edited by James B. Nickoloff. Minneapolis: Fortress, 1996.

———. *A Theology of Liberation: History, Politics, and Salvation.* Rev. ed. Translated and edited by Caridad Inda and John Eagleson. Maryknoll, N.Y.: Orbis Books, 1988.

Harvey, Van A. *A Handbook of Theological Terms.* New York: Macmillan, 1964.

Hellwig, Monika K. "Eschatology." Pages 340–72 in vol. 2 of *Systematic Theology: Roman Catholic Perspectives.* Edited by Francis Schüssler Fiorenza and John P. Galvin. Minneapolis: Fortress, 1991.

———. *Understanding Catholicism.* New York: Paulist Press, 1981.

———. *What Are They Saying about Death and Christian Hope?* New York: Paulist Press, 1978.

Hick, John. *Death and Eternal Life.* 1976. Repr., Louisville, Ky.: Westminster John Knox, 1994.

———. *Disputed Questions in Theology and the Philosophy of Religion.* New Haven: Yale University Press, 1993.

———. *A John Hick Reader.* Edited by Paul Badham. London: Macmillan Press Ltd., 1990.

———. *Problems of Religious Pluralism.* London: Macmillan Press Ltd., 1985.

Johnson, Elizabeth A. *Friends of God and Prophets: A Feminist Theological Reading of the Communion of Saints.* New York: Continuum, 1998.

Johnson, Roger. *Rudolf Bultmann: Interpreting Faith for the Modern Era.* San Francisco: Collins, 1987.

Kelly, J. N. D. *Early Christian Creeds.* 3d ed. New York: Longman, 1972.

Küng, Hans. *Credo: The Apostles' Creed Explained for Today.* Translated by John Bowden. New York: Doubleday, 1993.

————. *Eternal Life?* Translated by Edward Quinn. New York: Doubleday, 1985.

La Due, William. *Jesus among the Theologians: Contemporary Interpretations of Christ.* Harrisburg, Pa.: Trinity Press International, 2001.

The Last Things: Biblical and Theological Perspectives on Eschatology. Edited by Carl E. Braaten and Robert W. Jenson. Grand Rapids: Eerdmans, 2002.

Lohse, Bernhard. *Martin Luther: An Introduction to His Life and Work.* Translated by Robert C. Schultz. Philadelphia: Fortress, 1986.

Lossky, Vladimir. *The Mystical Theology of the Eastern Church.* 1st French ed. 1944. English trans. 1957. Repr., Crestwood, N.Y.: St. Vladimir's Seminary Press, 1976, 1998.

————. *The Vision of God.* Translated by Asheleigh Moorhouse. Crestwood, N.Y.: St. Vladimir's Seminary Press, 1963; repr. 1983.

Luz, Ulrich. *The Theology of the Book of Matthew.* Translated by J. Bradford Robinson. Cambridge: Cambridge University Press, 1996.

Macquarrie, John. *Christian Hope.* New York: Seabury Press, 1978.

————. *In Search of Humanity.* New York: Crossroad, 1985.

————. *Jesus Christ in Modern Thought.* Philadelphia: Trinity Press International, 1990.

————. *Thinking about God.* London: SCM Press, 1975.

Maximus the Confessor: Selected Writings. Translation and notes by George C. Berthold. Mahwah, N.J.: Paulist Press, 1985.

McManners, John. *Death and Enlightenment.* New York: Oxford University Press, 1981.

McNeill, John T. *The History and Character of Calvinism.* Oxford: Oxford University Press, 1967.

Meyendorff, John. *Byzantine Theology.* 2d ed. New York: Fordham University Press, 1987.

Moltmann, Jürgen. *The Coming of God: Christian Eschatology.* Translated by Margaret Kohl. Minneapolis: Fortress, 1996.

————. *Theology of Hope.* Translated by James W. Leitch. New York: Harper & Row, 1967.

Mussner, Franz. "The Synoptic Account of Jesus' Teaching on the Future Life." *Concilium* 66 (1970): 46–53.

Neuner, Josef, and Heinrich Ross. *The Teaching of the Catholic Church.* Edited by Karl Rahner. Translated by Geoffrey Stevens. New York: Alba House, 1967.

The New Oxford Annotated Bible with the Apocrypha. New Revised Standard Version. Edited by Bruce M. Metzger and Roland E. Murphy. New York: Oxford University Press, 1991.

Oberman, Heiko A. *Luther: Man between God and the Devil.* Translated by Eileen Walliser-Schwarzbart. New Haven: Yale University Press, 1989.

Pannenberg, Wolfhart. *The Apostles' Creed.* Translated by Margaret Kohl. Philadelphia: Westminster Press, 1972.

————. *Systematic Theology.* Vol. 3. Translated by Geoffrey W. Bromiley. Grand Rapids: Eerdmans, 1998.

Perrin, Norman. *The Promise of Bultmann.* New York: J. B. Lippincott, 1969.

The Philosophy of Kant: Immanuel Kant's Moral and Political Writings. Edited by Carl J. Friedrich. New York: Random House, 1949; repr. 1977.

Portalié, Eugène. *A Guide to the Thought of Saint Augustine.* Translated by Ralph J. Bastian. Westport, Conn.: Greenwood Press, 1960.

Rahner, Karl. "Eschatology." Pages 434–39 in *Encyclopedia of Theology: The Concise Sacramentum Mundi.* Edited by Karl Rahner. New York: Crossroad, 1975.

————. *Foundations of Christian Faith.* Translated by William V. Dych. New York: Crossroad, 1986.

————. "He Will Come Again." Translated by David Bourke. Pages 177–80 in vol. 7 of *Theological Investigations.* New York: Herder & Herder, 1971.

————. "The Hermeneutics of Eschatological Assertions." Translated by Kevin Smyth. Pages 323–46 in vol. 4 of *Theological Investigations.* Baltimore: Helicon Press, 1966.

————. "Last Things." Pages 821–22 in *Encyclopedia of Theology: The Concise Sacramentum Mundi.* Edited by Karl Rahner. New York: Crossroad, 1975.

————. "The Life of the Dead." Translated by Kevin Smyth. Pages 347–54 in vol. 4 of *Theological Investigations.* Baltimore: Helicon Press, 1966.

————. *On the Theology of Death.* Translated by Charles H. Henkey. New York: Herder & Herder, 1961.

————. "The Resurrection of the Body." Translated by Karl H. Kruger. Pages 203–16 in vol. 2 of *Theological Investigations.* Baltimore: Helicon Press, 1963.

Ratzinger, Joseph. *Eschatology—Death and Eternal Life.* Translated by Michael Waldstein. Edited by Aidan Nichols. Washington, D.C.: Catholic University of America Press, 1988.

Robinson, John A. T. *In the End, God . . . : A Study of the Christian Doctrine of the Last Things.* London: James Clarke, 1950.

————. *In the End God.* New York: Harper & Row, 1968.

————. *Jesus and His Coming.* Philadelphia: Westminster, 1979.

Ruether, Rosemary Radford. *Gaia and God: An Ecofeminist Theology of Earth Healing.* San Francisco: HarperSanFrancisco, 1992.

————. *Sexism and God-talk.* Boston: Beacon Press, 1983.

Sauter, Gerhard. *What Dare We Hope?* Harrisburg, Pa.: Trinity Press International, 1999.

Schillebeeckx, Edward. *Church: The Human Story of God.* Translated by John Bowden. New York: Crossroad, 1990.

Schleiermacher, Friedrich. *The Christian Faith.* Translated from the 2d German ed. by H. R. MacKintosh and J. S. Stewart. Edinburgh: T&T Clark, 1986.

Schwarz, Hans. *Eschatology.* Grand Rapids: Eerdmans, 2000.

Schweitzer, Albert. *The Mystery of the Kingdom of God.* Translated by Walter Lowrie. London: Adam & Charles Black, 1956.

————. *The Quest of the Historical Jesus.* Translated by W. Montgomery. New York: Macmillan, 1968.

Suchocki, Marjorie Hewitt. *The End of Evil: Process Eschatology in Historical Context.* Albany: State University of New York Press, 1988.

————. *God, Christ, Church.* New rev. ed. New York: Crossroad, 1989.

————. "Spirit in and through the World." Pages 173–90 in *Trinity in Process.* Edited by Joseph A. Bracken and Marjorie Hewitt Suchocki. New York: Continuum, 1997.

Taylor, Mark Kline. *Paul Tillich: Theologian of the Boundaries.* London: Collins, 1987.

Tillich, Paul. *Dynamics of Faith.* New York: Harper & Row, 1957.

————. *The New Being.* New York: Scribner's, 1955.

————. *The Shaking of the Foundations.* New York: Scribner's, 1948.

————. *Systematic Theology.* 3 vols. in 1. Chicago: University of Chicago Press, 1967.

Ware, Kallistos (Timothy). *The Inner Kingdom.* Vol. 1 of *The Collected Works.* Crestwood, N.Y.: St. Vladimir's Seminary Press, 2000.

Ware, Timothy (ordained Kallistos in 1966). *The Orthodox Church.* New York: Penguin Books, 1963; repr. with revisions 1993.

Witherington, Ben, III. *Jesus, Paul and the End of the World: A Comparative Study in New Testament Eschatology.* Downers Grove, Ill.: InterVarsity Press, 1992.

INDEX

eternal present of, 93
grace of, 53, 76
kingdom of
coming of, 6, 38–39, 62,
135–36
manifested in the church,
45
perfect community of,
27–29
love of
desires universal salvation,
48, 83–84, 123
infinite nature of, 104,
122, 133–34
is justice, 120
power of, 86, 103
revealed in Jesus Christ, 114
proof of existence of, 23, 69,
83, 94
will be "all in all," 3, 4, 10,
11, 72, 85, 134
God, Christ, Church (Suchocki),
119–20
God of the Oppressed (Cone),
136–37
Gospels. *See* Synoptic Gospels,
individual books of
Greek theology, ancient, 42, 47,
84, 95, 98, 121. *See also* Plato
Gregory of Nyssa
on punishment, 72, 78
on resurrection, 133
on universal salvation, 4,
10–11, 12, 132
Gutiérrez, Gustavo, 135–36

heaven
blessings of, 25, 73, 123, 143
communication between hell
and, 5–6, 14
freedom to choose, 64
physicality of, 36, 53, 72
as state of being, 21, 65, 71
See also reward; salvation

Heidegger, Martin, 92, 115
hell
communication between
heaven and, 5–6, 14
eternality vs. temporality of,
22, 25–26, 72, 77–78, 86,
122, 132
freedom to choose, 61, 64,
86, 133–34
have any humans been
consigned to?, 74, 78, 143
Jesus Christ's descent into,
70–71, 102, 114
torments of, 7, 14–15, 21,
22, 71
See also punishment;
purgatory; Sheol
Hellwig, Monika K., 73–76, 80
Helvetic Confession, Second, 101
Hick, John, 121–28
historicism, 26–27, 28–29
History of the Synoptic Tradition
(Bultmann), 35
Holy Spirit, 35, 41–43, 47, 70,
91–92, 94
hope, v, 109–16, 147
Hume, David, 23

immortality. *See* consciousness;
resurrection; soul
*Immortality of the Soul or
Resurrection of the Dead?*
(Cullmann), 42–43
Inner Kingdom, The (Ware), 133
Innocent IV, Pope, 16–17
In the End, God . . . (Robinson),
83–86
In Search of Humanity
(Macquarrie), 114–16
Irenaeus, 9, 10, 92
Isaiah, book of, 1, 71, 98, 101,
135, 140

Jeremiah, book of, 91, 121